MW00478991

BEGIN WITHIN

A Memoir of Self-Destructive Dating and Self-Discovering Divinity

Emma Hayes

Emma Hayes
*Begin Within: A Memoir of Self-Destructive Dating
and Self-Discovering Divinity*

ISBN-10: 1727311531
ISBN-13: 978-1727311532

Manufactured in the United States of America

Editor: Kristen van Vloten
Cover Illustration and Design: Mia Ohki
Interior Layout: Laura Wrubleski
Publishing Support: The Self Publishing Agency

To the girl I was.
And to you.

Introduction

Writing has always been a purifying experience for me. But around the time I abandoned myself (which we'll get to soon enough), I also deserted the one thing that helped me make sense of my world. Over a decade later, when I suddenly realized I was in the midst of a journey toward radical self-acceptance and unconditional self-love, I knew I needed to open myself back up to writing. And that's what *Begin Within* is: an assemblage of everything I've gone through and learned on a journey from, as my subtitle helpfully says, self-destructive dating to self-discovering divinity.

Have you ever heard the Hermetic principle *As Within, So Without*? It means that whatever is within directly correlates to that which is without, or that which is external or evident. I first heard the phrase back in 2016 and it immediately resonated with me. Everything that I had seen within myself always resembled what was outside of myself. It echoed on so many levels and clarified a lot of things I strove to understand.

But the most prominent evidence for the truth of this principle always popped up in my romantic relationships. When I struggled to see my worth, I attracted partners who made me feel unworthy. Not only that, but I knew I had a lot of restorative work that needed to be done. And instead of putting effort into loving and healing myself, I chose to put that intention into new relationships. For many years, I followed a pattern of searching outside of myself not only to find validation, acceptance, and love, but to avoid cultivating the light I had within me.

It's easy to hide behind things outside of ourselves so we can put off doing the internal work. But it's all going to be reflected back to us, whether we want to face it or not. Relationships were my go-to hiding places but everything I ran from still found me. My self-destructive tendencies were carefully curated, allowing me to search for love externally—and then if I didn't find it, I could feed the idea that I was unworthy of love. In turn, I continued to starve myself of my own love; a love I so desperately craved that had been available to me all along. It took a lot of vulnerability and compassion to take responsibility for nourishing my heart and tending my soul. When I finally faced my fear of loving myself wholly, I found it to be the most natural and magical legacy I had ever given myself.

I began writing *Begin Within* with the intention to simply get everything I was feeling out of my body. It was terrifying to face the unhealed parts of myself. I also knew I had a tendency to run from my healing the moment I made any progress. I wanted to be able to look back on this journey of discovering my own divinity with complete understanding and appreciation for my past experiences. The nostalgia I felt while looking back on my story soon shifted to a feeling of responsibility to share my experiences.

My hope is that this book encourages you to acknowledge the light already within you. You are whole. You are worthy. You are divine. Trust yourself and your magic. It is time to *Begin Within.*

CHAPTER ONE

Magic Sand

*T*his story starts like many others: girl meets boy.

In 2010, I began my first semester as a college student. After a couple weeks of learning how to manage classes and my work schedule, I ended up going to one of my co-workers' housewarming party. There I was, minding my single-lady business, when I noticed this very attractive, Henry Cavill look alike talking with one of my good friends. He looked familiar but I couldn't place him. I went to say hello to my friend and stuck out my hand to greet this blue-eyed babe. It turned out he was one of the morning shift leads, which explained why he looked familiar; he was usually leaving as I would come into work.

His name was Daniel. He was two years older than me and studying International Affairs. He was handsome, witty, and arguably too charming. My crush was instant.

Over the next few months, Daniel and I got to know each other as friends. We exchanged numbers and chit chatted at work if we ran into each other. Nothing too significant. But it was not lost on me the way I felt when I was around him. He was fascinating to me. He was clever and charismatic. He was a Renaissance man, knowing a lot about a lot. He was also one of the funniest people I had ever met. He always knew how to make me laugh. He had all of these qualities that I never knew I could find in one person.

It wasn't until my surprise birthday party that I realized how much I liked this guy. Several of my friends and I were at dinner before what was at that point still a surprise party, when suddenly my best friend Amber and Daniel said they had to leave. Amber mentioned she had plans already and Daniel said he needed to go do some homework.

It's my birthday and they aren't going to hang out with me? Also, who does homework on a Thursday?!

I was bummed. I really wanted to spend time with them, especially Daniel. But I kept the thought to myself, wishing them both a good night.

After dinner, the rest of my friends and I went to hang out at one of their apartments with the intention of watching a movie and having a quiet night in. Once I stepped through the door, thirty people screamed, "Surprise!" Streamers and balloons dotted the ceiling, a birthday cake was on the counter, and all of my friends—Daniel included—were in front of me. I was elated as I made my way around to hug everyone and take photos. When I got to Daniel, he gave me a mixed CD with handwritten notes about why he liked each song.

At that point, there was no going back; I was falling hard for this boy.

After my birthday party, we started officially hanging out. And it was a lot more awkward than I anticipated. Many of our early conversations revolved around his ex-girlfriend, a mutual friend he had taken on a date that didn't go anywhere, and the topic of other girls in general. It felt very strange getting to know someone who seemed to be more interested in other women's qualities rather than my own.

He mentioned to me often that he would have dreams with his ex-girlfriend in them. He seemed convinced that it meant he truly loved someone if they showed up in his dreams. He would then conveniently mention I was never in his dreams while detailing the ones with his ex-girlfriend. He explained to me how they were in love and how they dressed as Jim and Pam from *The Office* for Halloween. Comparison Train, ticket for one, please.

He also made me read their old messages from when they broke up, explaining that she had broken his heart. He told me a lot about her that I did not need to know. And none of it was especially kind. In fact, most of what he said me feel sorry for him, as if he had been the victim of some relationship that malfunctioned before it was supposed to. After he told me about his previous relationship, I did my best to make it known to him that I was not her. I wanted him to see me as *me*, not as a shadow of his ex-girlfriend.

There was one night when we were eating at a nice Italian restaurant that Daniel mentioned to me he had brought one of our co-workers there on a date. In passing he mentioned how he thought she might have been out of his league and that's why she stopped hanging out with him. What a strange thing to say to the girl you are hanging out with, who is obviously interested in you. I felt like he was insinuating that I was not his first choice. It was as though he wanted me to thank him for taking a chance on me. Then came the thoughts of, *Well, he's choosing to get to know me now so that's a good sign... Right?*

Once, he casually said to me, "Your roommate is *hot*." He wasn't lying. My roommate was beautiful. But I was surprised he said that to me considering he knew I liked him. And he was aware that she was seeing someone. That night in our dorm I asked her what she thought of Daniel and she nonchalantly responded, "Yeah, he's cute and seems funny."

A couple days later I told him what she had said and his face lit up. I put myself in such an uncomfortable position. I wanted him to feel complimented, but he was never happy unless those compliments came from another girl. It made me feel irrelevant. It seemed like he cared more about her opinion than he did mine just because he thought she was hot.

One night while hanging out at his apartment, he offered to move my car so I wouldn't get a ticket.

"Where are your keys?" he asked.

I nodded to the place they were resting on top of his dresser and he grabbed them.

"I'm going to move your car before it rains. And so you don't get a ticket," he said kindly.

"Thank you," I smiled at him. He kissed me on the forehead before heading out. He returned about ten minutes later, rain on his jacket. I thanked him again as he put my keys back on the dresser.

"Sure. You know? That's probably the nicest thing I've ever done for someone."

I thought maybe he was being humble. I didn't question his comment but I found it bizarre. Why would something so small stand out as being the nicest thing he had done for someone? I was aware he was not the most altruistic or generous person I knew. But I eventually found the reason he was so surprised at himself was because this kindness and selflessness was very out of character.

✳ ❄ ✳

By 2017, the year I sat down to write this, it had been seven years since I'd first met Daniel. From 2010 to 2016, I had been through the emotional ringer after years of unhealthy relationships. I had lost weight and gained it back. I was stuck creatively. I felt disconnected from the woman I wanted to become. I could feel my self-sabotaging tendencies creeping back up on me.

With New Year's 2017 approaching, I was inspired to dedicate the entire year to healing myself. I vowed to work through all the suppressed emotional traumas and outdated narratives that were holding me back.

I knew my suffering was self-created but I had held onto it for *so* long that I was afraid to let it go. I knew revisiting the past would force me to forgive the people I thought had done something wrong. More importantly, it would require me to forgive myself. This healing work would demand me to take full responsibility for my suffering in order to restore my soul. Unfortunately for me, this meant I needed to start by recalling my most unpleasant, and somehow most significant, relationships. And I was dreading it.

In 2010, about half a year before I met Daniel, I was a senior in high school, getting ready to graduate at the top of my class. I was headed to a good college and embracing the freedom to discover who I wanted to become. Although I was very much looking forward to this independence, I was also terrified.

Throughout my early life, I had been conditioned to follow other people's guidance rather than listen to my own intuition. I asked other people to give their input on everything. "Does this look good on me? Do you like this band? What color should I paint my room? Where are you applying for school? Where do you want to eat? What time did you want to go? What should I do? What do you think?"

I was practically screaming, "WHO SHOULD I BE?" as I waddled through life a follower. I can't recall any decisions that I made back then without someone else's input. I was beyond terrified of trusting myself with any decisions. Part of it was I didn't want to blame myself if anything went wrong. I was afraid of being proactive and also scared of taking responsibility for my own life.

Fear was one of the first and most common emotions I witnessed growing up. Fear of change. Fear of speaking up. Fear of being honest. Fear of the unknown. Fear of doing back flips on the trampoline.

The people around me unknowingly taught me to hold

fear in a higher regard than my intuition. And as I got older, I clung onto the familiarity that was fear.

One of my earliest memories is sleeping with my lamp on and forcing my parents to sprinkle "Magic Powder" around the edge of my bed to protect me. It was actually a bottle of glitter sand and they had never even opened the bottle. But I felt safer allowing the people around me to deal with my fear rather than facing it myself. Although I'm not sure how my parents could have gotten me to face my fear of the dark, or my fear of a crazy clown breaking in and murdering me. If they had *literally* made me face my fears by locking me in a dark room and hiring a clown, I probably would have been *more* afraid, even though it was just a simulation.

But fear is just that: a simulation. It puts blinders on us and can trick us into doing irrational things. Fear is a deception many of us have become so comfortable with that we are even afraid to release it. That's some cruel irony. I had allowed fear to dictate my entire life. I had been in the cycle so long that I didn't know how to function outside of fear. I had held onto fear so tightly that I eventually forgot why. And because I had been rooted in fear for so long, I couldn't see a way out. I remained in the fear cycle, as destructive as it was, simply because I found it familiar.

I knew going to college was the ideal chance for me to overcome this pattern. But the months between graduating high school and going to college felt like limbo. I was still caught in a fear cycle. I would feel inspired one day, and the next I would feel discouraged, like maybe I was making a mistake. Then, as with now, when I put too much time between the actions of facing my fears and taking a step forward into the unknown, I would backslide. I would purposefully give myself too much room. It allowed me to easily fall back into the fear cycle while ignoring my intuition. And I could blame something not working out on the timing being off or whatever other excuse I made up. I was just being too lazy and afraid of bettering myself. I was afraid of growing into who I was always meant to be.

Over the years I have found when I feel like doing something, I need to do it. When I start thinking, *Can I do it? I think I can do this,* that is my door. *That* is my chance to take a step forward without overthinking. But at 18 years old, I didn't know how to jump into the unknown. I only knew how to worry about the future. I was focused on the destination, not realizing how much clarity the journey would provide me. I was eager to open the door college was providing to find myself.

Two months into my freshman year, I desired a clean slate. I vowed to get fit and eat healthily. I wanted to find my life's purpose and choose a major that spoke to me. And I was genuinely adamant about not starting any new romantic relationships. I knew I wasn't ready to date anyone seriously. I was off at college. I wanted to focus on myself and my personal growth. I wanted to do what I wanted without having to split my focus between my self-growth and a partner.

But the second you make a promise to yourself the Universe gives you the opportunity to prove you meant it. And that's exactly what happened.

After our first kiss, Daniel drunkenly messaged me saying I was a terrible kisser. Then he quickly apologized, stating he shouldn't have said that. I was mortified. The guy I was really into didn't seem to care about my feelings, drunk or not. He apologized again in person but it had already been said. I wanted him to like me so much that I acted as if he hadn't hurt my feelings. I was more concerned about him feeling secure than exploring how poorly he made me feel.

One night at a friend's house party, I offered to go in and help the host clean up. The place was a disaster. I did the dishes in the sink, picked up some trash, and wiped down the kitchen counters. If you've ever been to a college house party, you know how gross it can get rather quickly. After I was done, we were sitting around with a circle of people playing Never Have I Ever. Daniel leaned over to me and said, "I can't tell if this is who you actually are."

I was taken aback by his comment. "What do you mean?"

"Like, doing the dishes and being…this nice, I guess."

"I'm not pretending," I said. It upset me that he thought I was pretending to be someone I wasn't. This short dialogue left me feeling uneasy. I felt like I was not enough for him. He had a way of successfully making me second-guess my authenticity.

Later that night, I ended up outside on the porch with Daniel and a couple other people. I had some beer left in my bottle and didn't want to drink it. I asked him if he wanted the rest. He laughed to himself and said, "You don't want the rest of your warm beer?" He drank it anyway. Before we went back inside he gently put his hands on my shoulders, looked me in the eyes and said, "The way your nose crinkles when you smile…it makes my heart melt."

It was the sweetest compliment I had ever been given. Suddenly my hurt feelings from earlier were gone. I was more concerned with his perception of me rather than figuring out how I felt about myself. Honestly, at that point I cared more about being with someone rather than making sure they were the right someone.

During the holidays he came and stayed with me at my parents' house. One night after getting out of the shower, I found he had lit candles for me in my room. It was a sweet gesture. Then he told me he had snooped through my nightstand drawers. I should have known he didn't just do something romantic for no reason. I found that anytime he would do something kind it was because he had to balance out whatever questionable action he had already taken or was going to take.

While peeping in my drawers, he came across a draft I had written in high school. It was titled: My Dream Man. I had listed all of the things that I desired in a boyfriend on a piece of paper after a church camp. These are a few of the things I can remember from that list: loved God, kind, handsome, funny, would watch my favorite movies, would comfort me, would let me put my cold feet on him, and always made me feel loved.

Daniel said to me, "Emma, I'm not any of these things."

I thought perhaps his previous relationship had caused him to believe he wasn't good enough. I gave him words of encouragement. I told him he was who I wanted to be with. I explained that what I wanted in a partner now wasn't reflected on that old list. I told him I had made that list a long time ago and I knew it was a lot to ask for.

This was the moment I stopped believing that someone would be right for me. It didn't take much to convince me that there was no such thing as The One.

We had stopped at his house on our way back to campus when he asked to see my laptop. He got on my Facebook and suddenly I was no longer listed as single but in a relationship. Don't get me wrong, I was elated that he was making a public commitment to me. I had never received that reassurance from him before. But it didn't make me feel special. I wasn't directly involved in that moment of us deciding we were going to be a couple.

A few days after becoming "official", we had sex. It was my first time. We had talked about it before. He wasn't a virgin; I was. I remember him telling me, "I really think you'd like it."

And I was tired of waiting. I told him I was ready. He asked me if I was sure and I said yes. It was mediocre at best. Maybe I had hyped it up. I at least thought my first time would feel special. But it was neither special nor romantic. It was not at all how I had imagined my first time would be. Feeling a bit disappointed, I asked Daniel if we could cuddle. He stood up, reached for his shirt, and said, "I don't like cuddling." With his shirt back on, he returned to his desk and continued playing on his computer.

A few days later, before classes were due to start up again, there was a severe snowstorm. My friends and I decided to make an event of it. We packed up our clothes and games to stay at our friends' apartment. Daniel barely made it there before the roads were too bad to drive. We were stuck there for a few days. We walked a mile and back to the store to buy hot chocolate and made soup and grilled cheeses for ten people. Despite the rough weather, it felt magical.

I'm a Scorpio. I am deeply sensitive. And I find snow enchanting. All I wanted was to have a significant moment with Daniel. I wanted some reassurance that we were on the same page, especially considering we had recently slept together. That never happened. Instead, in that dark living room, while everyone was sleeping, we sat with each other at the kitchen table. We were talking about our relationship. I may have said something like I felt so close to him, blah blah blah. I don't remember what I mentioned but it doesn't matter. What came out of his mouth that night would eclipse anything else that was said.

"I'm never going to be in love with you so if you want to break up, I understand," he said flatly.

I felt my body go cold. What do you say to someone who has decided they will never love you? I don't remember what my response was. But I remember reassuring myself that love takes time.

I felt like nothing I did for him made him happy. But instead of bringing it up, I pushed aside my feelings and tried even harder. It seemed the more I tried to express my feelings, the more rejection I was met with.

For most of the spring semester, I stayed at his place. There was one night when all I wanted was to cuddle with him. He hesitated but obliged. He lay with me with his arm around my shoulder for about ten minutes on the sofa before claiming to be ready for bed. He then blew up the air mattress for me before saying goodnight as he went to his room.

I got ready for bed in silence. I took my contacts out, moved my blanket to the air mattress, and tucked myself in. I could feel the tears coming. I gave in, crying as quietly as I could into the pillow. I heard his door open and him walk over to me. He crouched down, hand on my shoulder, asking me what was wrong. There was so much I wanted to say, like, *I wanted to have this quality time with you and you just went to bed. I feel like nothing I do makes you happy. Sometimes I feel like you don't actually like me. In fact, I feel like you don't even want me here.*

Instead, all I could muster saying was, "You didn't even kiss me goodnight."

He sat in silence before kissing me on the forehead. Then as quickly as he had come out he went back to his room. I could have expanded on how much this instance hurt me but I didn't. Instead I fell asleep on a tear soaked pillow 20 feet from a guy that made me feel unworthy.

I have never been great at expressing my feelings. Growing up, I was never encouraged to express how I felt. And if I did, it usually was not met with much empathy, or even acknowledgement. So I came to view emotions as a sickness, something you should silently experience but not talk about. Whenever I felt like sharing my feelings, I would get anxious and a pit would form in my stomach. I was embarrassed for having feelings that differed from those around me.

I didn't have an example to look to when it came to healthily expressing my emotions. I mimicked how the adults in my life were acting. I either waited too long and my emotions spluttered out in a mess of tears or I locked myself in my room, swallowing the pain I wanted to release.

But I had been deluded by too many romantic comedies. I thought the harder it was, and the more effort I put in, meant things would turn out better than if it hadn't been difficult at all.

I figured the perfect way to reconnect would be to get away for a few days. We ended up going to a quiet beach for spring break. I was looking forward to spending some quality time together in a relaxed environment with no air mattress. But instead of the recharging trip I'd imagined, it was rather unpleasant. He complained about my taste in music, saying it was all the same. He took his laptop with him everywhere, to the point where we sat on sidewalks so he could use it.

One night at the hotel, we were eating the last of our groceries. I had opened something and he stared at me. "Do you want some?"

"You're still hungry?" he asked in disbelief.

"Yeah..." I said through red cheeks. He kept staring at me, almost as if he was waiting on me to say, *Gotcha! Of course I'm not hungry after eating two strawberries and half a granola bar!*

He laughed to himself, although it came across as laughing at me, and said, "Okay," before finishing his food.

Then the sour cherry on top: he didn't want to use this alone time to be intimate. Instead, he designated one bed as his own and left the other one to me. We were on vacation, in our own hotel room, and he chose to be on his laptop instead of spending the time *together*.

The morning we were leaving he apologized for not wanting to be intimate. I didn't want to get into an argument so I told him it was fine. That couldn't have been farther from the truth. I felt the only way I could connect with him was physically. So him saying he didn't want to be intimate made me feel more disconnected and unwanted than ever.

On our way back from the beach, we had gotten a little lost. One of the road signs had a different name than the one listed in our directions. I was talking out loud, saying I thought it was the right road but maybe we should stop and ask for directions.

"Calm the fuck down," Daniel said harshly.

His words stung. I grew up around adults who would curse at each other and speak unkindly to each other. I hated it. I knew that was something I would *never* accept from a partner. I gathered my thoughts while holding back tears and staring out the window. He eventually pulled up to a gas station for us to ask directions. Before getting out, I looked at him and said, "Don't ever speak to me that way again."

Despite the horror that was spring break, when we got back to college I told him I was in love with him.

I was sitting on his couch, his back to me as he hunched

over his desk.

"Can I tell you something?"

The look on his face told me he knew what I was about to say. He remained in his chair but turned to face me. "Emma…"

"I love you and just need you to know," I said, looking down at my hands.

He came over and sat by me, saying, "I really like you."

I smiled wanly. I knew what he was implying. "I just needed you to know," I said quietly.

He sighed. "You don't love me," he replied tiredly.

A few weeks later I found a message he had sent a mutual friend the same night I told him I loved him.

Daniel: Can I talk to you, man? You've been in a relationship a while and I just need some clarity.

Bryan: Sure, man, what's up?

Daniel: Emma's over here asleep. And I'm just feeling like shit because I know I'm never going to love her.

Bryan: Have you told her?

Daniel: Yeah.

Bryan: I think the right thing to do would be to end things with her if you're not feeling it.

Daniel: Thanks man.

These weeks-old messages brought me to immediate tears. I left my class early to sob in the privacy of a bathroom stall. I cried until I couldn't anymore. (Shout out to that sweet girl who asked me if I wanted to borrow her mascara: women like you are true heroes.)

I was heartbroken. Daniel was never going to reciprocate my feelings. I fell back into the thought pattern that something was wrong with me. I thought, *If my partner isn't feeling as strongly as I am, then maybe I'm not meant to have a partner who fully reciprocates my feelings.* I thought that with time he would come to love me. But he had already decided he wouldn't. I felt used and worthless. I was a body to him, someone to hook up with but not someone he wanted to connect with on a deeper level. I felt unlovable and almost ashamed of myself. I had given every part of me to this guy who was never invested in me.

And yet I stayed with him.

※ 十 ※ ·-

Over the summer we played trivia with his friends. There was one night a girl I had never met before joined us. She was an International Affairs major like all of them and had decided to join since her other plans had fallen through. As she made her way to a chair, Daniel's closest friend Robby said, "Haley is here. It's time to make your move."

Um, did he forget I was there? Daniel laughed at his friend's comment, face blushing. It was as if he just got called out on having a crush in front of his crush. While hanging outside before everyone left, I decided to pull Daniel aside. I wanted to address how I felt rather than not say anything *again*. I told him how his friend's comment was offensive and hurtful.

He tried brushing it off, saying it was just a joke. But *I* felt like the joke. I tried explaining to him that I didn't find it funny. But he just wasn't getting it. So I told him to go get her. I certainly wasn't being serious, but he responded, "Emma, I could never get a girl like that."

"A girl like *that*?" I echoed.

"You know what I mean…"

We both knew what he was saying. Haley was slim and beautiful. I was just the bigger girl with a cute nose. He only ever cared about looks. I shouldn't have been surprised by his comment. And I wasn't. I was devastated.

But nothing changed. Fall semester was on its way. The normalcy of having a routine comforted me. I thought Daniel and I could get back into the swing of things and we would be fine. The entire week before classes started something felt off. There seemed to be more distance between us. I felt like he didn't even want to be around me anymore.

In the car one night, I decided to say something.

"Sometimes I feel like you don't even like me," I said, breaking the silence with the thought that had taken up residence in my mind over the last several months.

Daniel didn't try to persuade me into believing I was wrong. I told him I thought he did love me, or could love me, but was too afraid to fall. He assured me he was not in love with me and never would be.

There was nothing else I could say. I had been holding onto this relationship, hoping that one day he would come to care for me the way I did for him. I believed in his potential for love like it was a bottle of magic sand. And of course, the lid never even came off. It never happened, and it was never going to happen. He had told me this from the beginning. I disregarded every red flag along the way in the hopes that I could create my own destiny. He had committed to the idea that he would never be happy with me. I was tired of waiting for him to allow us to work. It didn't feel like a relationship anymore.

It was time for me to move on.

The next day, he came over to talk. He sighed, "Let's get back together." I won't ever forget the tone behind it. It was as if he didn't actually agree with what he was saying and yet that didn't stop him. I went along with it, agreeing to get back together. That lasted for a total of two hours. We went out to the store and once I pulled back up to my apartment, he said, "I can't do this."

I was pissed. I said I didn't think he was as upset as I was to which he replied that he had cried the day before. But even when he brought that up, it felt like he was only saying it to convince me he was upset. Or maybe he was trying to convince himself?

I'll never know.

CHAPTER TWO

One Step Forward, Two Steps Back

Following the break up, Daniel and I still had to see each other a lot. Our work schedules overlapped more than they had in the spring. It was not easy. I could tell he was putting in effort to be especially kind to me. *Why is he putting more effort into being friends than he ever did when we were together?*

Then he started with the declarations of wanting to remain friends. So not only did I have to see him almost every day, but I had to endure hearing him explain how he wanted to keep our friendship. I didn't want either of these things. I didn't want to keep seeing his face, forced-smiling at me. I did not want to hear another word about how he "valued" my friendship. I wanted the space that should be allowed after any heavy breakup but I was not given that luxury.

After another run in mixed with fake pleasantries, I couldn't hold it in any longer.

"I have no interest in being your friend right now," I said through frustration. "I don't want you to keep smiling at me, acting like this whole mess never happened. You're putting more effort into me now than you did during our entire relationship. *You* broke *my* heart. You don't get to be my friend after that."

The distance didn't last long. I had a hard time being apart from him. After months of spending practically every day together, I missed his companionship. I missed his sense of humor. I thought that perhaps we had been friends all along but I had been pushing for more. Although he was not friendly and warm towards me during our relationship, I liked the freedom that our friendship fostered. There were no expectations. The hurt was still there but I knew to tread with caution.

About a month after we broke up, I went on a date with a friend of a friend. Daniel was hanging out at my apartment and I told him I had to run to the store. Guy and I went to dinner and had a decent time. By the end of the date, I knew nothing was going to happen between us. I think I knew that even before we went on the date. I just wanted to get my mind off of Daniel. I wanted to convince myself I was over him.

When I got back to my apartment, Daniel wasn't there. It turns out someone had let slip that I was on a date and he bolted. I felt pangs of guilt as I fell asleep that night, not only for lying, but for (I assumed) causing him any amount of pain.

It was easy to maintain space after the date fiasco. We were able to avoid seeing each other at work. But we stayed in touch. We were both struggling with the break up, the distance, and how to move forward. There was a lot of resentment on my end, feeling as though I had been led on and treated as nothing more than a friend with benefits the entirety of our relationship. I was dealing with feeling unworthy and unlovable. There were a lot of emotions I needed to work through that had only surfaced because of my relationship with Daniel.

By the middle of fall semester, we hadn't seen or spoken to each other in weeks. I was glad to finally have the space to process my emotions without him around to make me feel guilty for moving forward with my life.

One weekend my roommates and I went to a friend's house party. The host was friends with Daniel as well but I was assured ahead of time that he would not be there. After a couple drinks, I made my way upstairs to say hello to their cat. The bathroom door was shut and the light was on inside but I didn't think anything of it. I sat on the bed petting the cat when suddenly Daniel opened the bathroom door.

"Look who it is," he said, unsurprised, bitterness laced in his voice. I could tell he was already a couple drinks in. He was smiling to himself not out of joy but what seemed like victory. As if my obvious discomfort at seeing him at a party I was told he would *not* be at meant he had won the made up contest of who was successfully moving on.

"I didn't know you were going to be here," I responded, avoiding eye contact.

"Obviously," he said flippantly.

He left the room and the tears quickly followed. As one of those rare creatures who experiences tears with the majority of her emotions, I had to give them the space to arrive and depart on their own terms. I eventually made my way back downstairs and after another drink found myself on the front porch. There's something about being under the night sky that has always provided me calmness and clarity. While I sat, pondering whether I should find a ride home or stay until my group was ready to leave, the front door opened.

I turned around to see Daniel. He made his way slowly over to me and sat down by me on the steps. We sat in silence for a few minutes. I had nothing really to say to him. And I certainly did not want to hear anything he had to say.

He spoke up first.

"What are you doing out here?" he snarled disinterestedly.

"I wanted some air," I responded, looking down at my cup. "This is really hard," I confessed. I was hoping my vulnerability, this crack that showed how deeply I was struggling with the loss of our relationship, would stir some compassion in both of us. I didn't want to see him in pain. I assumed he felt the same way about me but his abrupt laugh told me otherwise.

"This is *hard* for you?" he asked mockingly and in disbelief. He laughed again to the side, looking up at the sky as if waiting for the joke to be over.

I felt immediately sober and stunned at his brashness. "Yes," I said in the most convincing tone I could muster. I looked at him, the witty, intelligent, hypnotic blue-eyed boy that I had fallen for, and someone I had never seen before quickly replaced him.

He whipped around to face me and shouted, "Hard for you?" I watched his eyes widen as he continued yelling. "Tell me how this is hard for you! This isn't *hard* for you!"

he sneered. "Did you look up how to kill yourself today? I LOOKED UP HOW TO KILL MYSELF TODAY!"

I felt my face go white and I began sobbing.

"Why are *you* crying?" he asked, sounding repulsed. He had become strangely composed. "Did *you* look up how to kill yourself today?" he questioned arrogantly. "Because I did," he said, suddenly and eerily calm. I felt like I was no longer in my body. It was as though I was watching this entire scene outside of myself.

I was speechless. My body tensed up as I continued crying. Then someone I'd never met before appeared in front of us and escorted Daniel inside. He had heard the entire exchange. He promised me he would make sure Daniel got home safely. Then he grabbed my designated driver and asked her to take me home. As soon as I hit my bed, I fell asleep.

When I woke up, the previous night's events started flooding back in. I texted Daniel to see how he was doing. Hours later I had still not heard back from him. I called but there was no answer. By late afternoon I began to fear the worst. We hadn't reached the point yet where we didn't respond to each other's texts or calls. Having not heard from him all day, I felt I had no other choice but to call his mom. I told her what he had said about harming himself and that I was worried because I couldn't get in touch in him.

She drove to his house, waking him up to talk about what I had disclosed to her. He was pissed. "This is just what I need," he texted me.

About an hour later, he called me and asked if he could come over. Feeling a responsibility to him, I said of course.

Once he got there, he told me how the intervention had gone. His mom had shown up crying, along with two deputies. They talked to him about seeking help. And they asked him if there was anyone he felt safe to spend time with.

He said me.

I was the person he trusted most to keep him safe. *I* was the person he wanted to spend time with. *I* was the person whom he felt would make his days easier.

I was suddenly entrusted with spending most of every day with him; going to the grocery store, to the movies, and just keeping him busy to keep his mind off of everything he was dealing with internally. This went on for about a week. After that, he went on to see a therapist and we resumed minimal contact.

Two weeks after he had started his therapy sessions, he called to tell me how great he was feeling.

"I told my therapist that I loved you, by the way," he said boastfully.

With as much compassion as I could gather, I said, "Daniel, I'm really glad you're feeling better. But that doesn't mean anything now."

"I thought you would like that. I just thought it was cool that I said it," he replied.

"And like I said, I'm really glad that you're finding the answers you were looking for. I'm so happy that you're feeling better. But saying that now doesn't change anything. It doesn't take back everything that's already been said. That's not a resolution I was expecting or wanting if I'm honest. I'm just glad you are feeling better."

It was true, on all counts. I was relieved that he was feeling better. I never wanted to see him hurting. But this revelation he had about actually being in love with me the entire time did nothing but cause me more pain. After hearing the lightness in his voice, I convinced myself to go see a professional as well.

My therapist Angelica was a fierce and beautiful African woman. She had lovely hip-length braids and always sported brightly colored lipstick. She was so unbelievably sure of herself. I thought, *I want to be like that.* She was strong and full of gentleness and compassion. She was also quite candid. She did not encourage my initial self-deprecating humor. Rather she would watch me patiently, slightly smiling, and wait for me to restate whatever I had just said but with more self-compassion.

During our sessions, Angelica gave me exercises to do, like pointing out what I loved about myself. It was difficult at first. I had never taken the time to evaluate who I was or speak so kindly to myself. She created a safe space for me to completely love myself without shame or judgment. Once I saw that she was never going to judge me harder than I had judged myself, I opened up about feeling unworthy and not good enough. I felt very comfortable sharing all my struggles that had magnified over the last year.

I told her all about my relationship with Daniel as objectively as I could. I didn't want to feel like I was talking shit about him but I wanted to get everything I was feeling out of me. I shared with her the lack of acceptance I felt growing up. I expressed feeling guilty about when my dog had been hit by a car. I opened up about my struggle with self-love because I didn't feel recognized or supported by those around me. In my mind, if I didn't feel those things from the people around me then I should not be allowed to feel them about myself.

Angelica was the most patient adult I had ever met. She let me talk until I had nothing left to say. She actively listened to me. And when I would ask her questions, hoping for a professional answer, she would reroute my questions back to me so I could find my own answers.

She also had me do a lot of self-awareness exercises. She would give me lists with 10-20 adjectives and have me circle 5 that described me. A few times I would circle an adjective that did not truly describe me. My Old Self thought self-deprecation was a funny way to express what she didn't like about herself. But my therapist never played that game.

Angelica would take the piece of paper and squint at the one word that didn't belong with the other four I had circled. She would look up at me and, unconvinced, ask, "Ugly?" or "Unintelligent?" or "Idiotic?" or whatever word it was that obviously did not describe me.

After a couple sessions of this, she began having me write my own lists. I would always have to start by writing what I loved most about myself. I always had something kind to say about myself; all I had needed was a safe space to do so. She introduced me to positive affirmations, which are still fundamental to my self-care routine.

Angelica also helped me work through my feelings of

shame for going to see her in the first place. I thought I was weak for being unable to work through my emotions on my own. I felt like my thoughts and feelings weren't valid because I was the only one experiencing them. She assured me that I was allowed to feel any emotions that come up. She helped me navigate through my thoughts and emotions without attachment or judgment. I was allowed to feel them but learned how not to hold onto them.

Angelica described it like Alice in Wonderland falling down that rabbit hole. I had the choice to try and grab onto the wall (my thoughts) or to acknowledge them and move forward without attachment or opposition.

After a while, I finally realized that my relationship with Daniel was not good for my mental or emotional health. This was a difficult conclusion. I felt I had wasted time investing in a relationship that did not prove to be healthy or good for me. I was worried about how other people regarded the break up as well. Did they think I was naive for not ending it sooner? Or were they proud of me for finally seeing how bad that relationship was for me?

Either way, I still felt like I had failed.

If you need to talk to someone, please call 1-800-273-TALK
or visit www.iasp.info/resources for your nation's hotline number.
Every struggle is different but you are not alone.

CHAPTER THREE

Tripping

After several therapy sessions, I felt like I was ready to stand on my own two feet again. Daniel and I stayed in contact, still having to see each other at work occasionally. He said he felt a lot better and we never spoke of the porch incident again.

After a month of maintaining an actual friendship with Daniel, he easily convinced me that we could hook up without any repercussions. I knew deep down that if I agreed, I would be taking a billion steps backward from all the work I had done to move on. But he was so...convincing? Charming? His blue eyes always had this glint like he knew better than I did. I thought I was prepared to keep moving forward but the second I got the chance, I fell right back to where I had been a few months prior.

We continued on through the fall semester as friends with benefits. But I didn't feel like I was gaining anything from the arrangement. I had given myself the role of his support system so I kept putting myself back into his arms. He made me think that being there for him in that capacity was how he would best heal. I held onto the hope that if we worked on ourselves outside of a recognized relationship that we might make our way back to each other. I quickly found that I was only putting myself in a position to be used. Any time we would hook up he would ignore me for days, sometimes weeks, afterwards. It was like breaking up all over again. I gave until I had nothing else to give, even to myself.

Sometime after the holidays, Daniel stopped talking to me. Over the course of six months he had become a stranger. I didn't see him around work anymore. Anytime I texted him or called, he did not answer. Initially I was worried, replaying the porch scene in my head. But mutual friends told me that he seemed to be doing well.

I was happy for him. All I had wanted was for him to be feeling better. But it left me feeling like I meant nothing to him. He wanted to keep hooking up until he felt good enough about himself to go back out into the dating scene. It infuriated me. I felt unappreciated and used, no better than a tissue tossed in the trash after his solo time. And, worst of all, after a year of identifying myself with Daniel I felt lost when he was no longer a part of my life.

✴ ⼘ ✸ ⼀

I decided to spend that summer in my hometown. It didn't take long to find a distraction. Connor was cute enough but he was certainly not my type. He had dropped out of high school and was unemployed. He had a thick Southern accent that was hard to understand. And that's saying a lot because I grew up around the good ol' Southern drawl. He also partook in celebrating the green every day, multiple times a day.

Aside from all the things I did not like about him, he brought out a lot of good in me. He helped me to stop taking myself so seriously and coaxed me out of my shell. I liked that he always made it clear how he felt about me. He actively put in effort to spend time with me.

I had a lot fun with Connor that summer. We went swimming and to the movies. We cooked together and went out to restaurants. We binge-watched *Ghost Adventures* and *Impractical Jokers*. He had an old convertible and almost every night we would drive with the top down while the sun was setting.

All of that sounds romantic, and I'm sure for him it was. But Connor was my distraction from all the pain I was ignoring. I felt safe to be vulnerable with him because I didn't reciprocate his feelings.

All my relationship with Connor did was highlight the things I missed about Daniel. The more time I spent with Connor, the more I thought about Daniel. I hadn't gotten the closure I needed to truly move on. Or at least that's what I told myself. So I decided to write Daniel a letter. He wouldn't answer my phone calls or texts and I wanted to get everything I was feeling out of me. And this was the only way I knew how.

I wrote that I missed him and still cared about him. I touched on all of the small things that I missed, like the way he would rub his feet together before falling asleep. Stuff that might seem insignificant or silly to someone else were things I couldn't shake. I told him I was sorry for everything that had happened over the last year. And I told him I truly hoped he was happy.

I never expected a response so I was surprised when a few weeks later his name popped up on my phone.

It wasn't a pleasant conversation.

He said it was pathetic of me to write him a letter when it was obvious he had been intentionally ignoring me. He said I didn't really miss him. He mentioned he had seen one of my tweets about wanting to be a Public Relations major; he said I wasn't likeable enough to have that job. He said I should just stick with becoming a teacher because that was more fitting for me. He told me that if I worked on myself hard enough *maybe* I could find someone to love me. He said that only if I lost weight could I be happy and find someone to be with. The box he had so carefully curated for me during our relationship was back out. Every word out of his mouth cracked my heart like a whip: painful, cruel, merciless. I was stunned into silence and began crying.

"Please don't cry," he begged.

It was like someone punching you and saying, *Don't get a bruise.*

"It was good to hear from you," I breathed in sharply, pulling myself together. "I've got to go though," I rushed, quickly hanging up.

⁜ ⁜ ⁜

After that phone call, I didn't know what to do anymore.

I had blindly trusted someone else with my feelings and my energy which left me empty. I felt like no one was ever going to love me. I had been in a relationship with someone who, for months, was only ever there physically and not emotionally. I thought that was all I was ever going to get from a relationship so I accepted that as my truth.

Rather than spending the summer healing myself, I just dove right back into my summer fling. I sought comfort in the first person who gave me attention. I wasn't going to be picky about who I dated at that point. I just wanted to cleanse my palate of Daniel.

Before even getting involved with Connor, I had already decided that I wasn't going to let myself fall. That's where everything had gone wrong in my relationship with Daniel. I was convinced emotional intimacy was too toxic for me to have in my future relationships. I settled on the idea that I was never going to find someone who met all of my needs. Once I believed that, it didn't take long for my reality to reflect how I felt on the inside.

When school started back, I inevitably ended things with Connor. He told me he loved me and I told him he didn't. Doesn't this sound familiar? My relationship with Daniel had emotionally traumatized me. Every positive and negative experience I had with him somehow bled through many of the relationships I had. I would either let myself get too close or I would keep my heart at a distance. The only previous dating experience I had at that point was my high school boyfriend and Daniel. So I had experienced two extremes: one young, high school love and one emotionally toxic relationship. I didn't know what it felt like to have an adult relationship that was healthy and balanced.

That fall I kept myself busy. I focused on my classes and cultivating my friendships. I had moved into a new house with two great friends. I was fostering a puppy. Even though I had to endure seeing Daniel occasionally at work, I was doing really well.

Well, that all went to hell around the holidays. 'Tis the season!

At our office holiday party, Daniel approached me after months of not speaking.

"Emma, can I talk to you?"

"When I'm done."

I finished up taking pictures and he led me aside. He said, "You look great. You look…happy…"

"Thank you. I am," I said lightly. He seemed disappointed by my response.

After my friends and I sat down, Daniel was walking around looking for a place to sit. No one had saved him a spot. He was visibly upset. I told him he could sit with us but he declined. He left before the party even started.

I've never been great at expressing my emotions, but I've always been exceptionally gifted at feeling them. My friends could tell I was unsettled over Daniel leaving. They reminded me that I wasn't responsible for him. They told me it was his choice to leave. And I heard what they were saying. It was not my job to convince him to stay. I was not responsible for his feelings.

But after the banquet was over, I asked a server if I could take a plate of food to my friend who had to leave early. I texted Daniel, making sure it was okay to come over. He seemed grateful. After he ate he came over to me, grinned, and suggested we have sex. I told him I didn't really want to. I knew that if we did, I would get my hopes up. But I gave in. It made me feel sadder than I thought I could.

✳ ┼ ✳ ┼

Fast forward almost a year. Summer had ended, classes started back, and I had the pleasure of seeing Daniel date a coworker. Alicia resembled Zoe Saldana but had the personality of Tina Fey. She was beautiful, kind, and witty. We weren't exceptionally close but I knew her. It was very strange having to be in such close proximity to their blossoming relationship. Aside from the obvious—that I didn't enjoy having a front row seat to their relationship—seeing them together bothered me tremendously. But it took weeks to figure out why.

It wasn't that I had to see them together during the week. It wasn't that she was noticeably more in shape than I was. And, believe it or not, it was not that I was jealous or interested in *ever* being with him again. There was some reason that made seeing them remarkably painful and I wanted to figure it out.

When you go looking for an answer, sometimes it is not gentle with the delivery. And my answer was like a slap in the face.

There was one afternoon when we all got off work at the

same time. The two of them were in front of me as I walked to my car. Suddenly, I saw Daniel take her bag and sling it over his shoulder.

That gesture might have seemed meaningless to an outsider but it said a lot to me. Daniel had never done something that small and selfless for me, aside from moving my car that one time. It was difficult to see someone who showed an abnormal lack of effort with me to be actively doing kind things in his new relationship. I wanted to be happy that maybe he had changed. I was also totally pissed off that he waited until after we broke up to be a good boyfriend. The more I compared how he had been with me to what I saw between them, the worse I felt.

I briskly walked to my car before the waves of emotion could knock me over. I sat and watched them pull out of the parking lot before sobbing. Remember when I said I am someone who greets the majority of her emotions with tears? I was not exaggerating. It's still difficult to say if I had been more sad or more mad.

I called my mom, hoping she would give some soothing words of advice. But unlike me, my mom is not overly sensitive. I'm still not sure who I got the trait from. My mom is stoic and if she's not being blunt then she's not talking. It's one of the things I appreciate most about her; she doesn't waste her words. But sometimes I just need someone to talk things out with me.

After listening to me blubber, she asked, "Are you about to start your period?" It was one of the most prominent examples of internalized sexism that my family enjoys using to explain any woman being emotional. But that's a different conversation for perhaps another book.

In her own way, I know she was trying to get me to see my sadness as a byproduct of my moon cycle and *not* because I had allowed some boy to make me upset. But I was allowed to feel my emotions and give them the space they required in order to move forward regardless of my moon cycle. I wanted to express how I was feeling. It fazed me to see someone I had invested effort into—who did not reciprocate said effort—doing that for someone else.

My mom listened to me as I talked out my emotions until I came to the conclusion that no one was to blame. How Daniel was with his new girl had nothing to do with me, so I shouldn't let it affect me.

My mom continued to listen as I composed myself. Once it was apparent I had nothing else to say she gently said, "Go home and get some sleep." And I did.

✳ ⁌ ✳ ⁌

The next morning I woke up hungover from the emotional night before. I was still hurting. I didn't know how to help the large, unhealed part of myself that I was left with. But instead of wallowing, which I wanted to do, I put on my boss bitch pants and continued moving forward.

I kept to myself, going to class and hanging out with my small group of friends. I didn't go out as much, instead preferring to stay home and watch documentaries about plant-based eating. I took those next several months to heal and release all of the negative energy I had been holding onto. I realized who Daniel had been had nothing to do with me. And along the way I forgave him. Now, my forgiveness didn't mean I accepted his poor behavior. Forgiveness is releasing a self-created attachment that is no longer serving you. It's about releasing you from suffering in order to regain your peace. And don't be mistaken. Forgiveness is not a "one and done" thing. If your memory is still emotionally charged, you must forgive again.

This happened a little bit at a time. I realized I shouldn't take any of Daniel's actions or words personally. It was hard to come to terms with because I had no one to blame for how I felt except myself. He had been projecting his insecurities onto me and I had been projecting mine onto him. Neither of us was whole when we began our relationship.

Growing up, we're all told that our perfect half is out there. It always rubbed me the wrong way, feeling like I had to dim myself in order for someone else to light me up. As if it was someone else's destiny to make me whole rather than my own. I was lead to believe I could only ever reach my full potential if I had a partner. I was under the impression that you had to be broken before you could be fulfilled; that the fulfillment you were seeking could only be found outside of yourself. I never thought too hard about it, trusting those who used the phrase. I was under the impression that someone else would fulfill me, not that I had the ability to fulfill myself. I allowed those around me to determine what I was worth.

My relationship with Daniel controlled how I defined

myself. And without it I felt lost. I never knew who I was on my own. That's why I had been so excited about college. I was too focused on what we could be and not who we were, especially as individuals. I never figured out who I wanted to be as my own person. Once I became aware of this tendency, I felt a gentle wave of peace. I knew I had the capacity to stop giving my power to people who didn't care about me or my heart.

⁂

That spring my job chose about thirty staff members to go to a business conference in Buffalo, NY for a week. It was going to be my first plane ride and I'd never been up north. I was pumped because my other best friend, Emily, was getting to go as well.

I scanned the email for who else would be going and there he was: Daniel Wheeler. I immediately felt nauseous. For a blissful moment, I had forgotten there was even a possibility of him being on this trip. I also, up until that moment, thought I had been doing really well. I had been releasing residual feelings from the relationship and taking the time to heal my heart. Yet knowing he would be on the trip knocked the wind out of me.

I was sitting in the boarding area when Daniel approached me.

"You excited?" he asked.

I was caught off guard. I had been hoping to avoid him on this trip. "Yeah, it's my first time going on a plane."

"No it's not," he said skeptically.

"Yes, it is. You know I've never been on a plane," I said.

He didn't respond.

Even though it was a business trip, we ended up having a lot of down time. One late morning after getting back from the conference, a few of my coworkers and I were playing cards in the lobby. Without knowing why, I looked up and saw it snowing outside the glass doors. We all hurried outside and stood on the sidewalk, looking up to the grey sky sending down flurries. Almost as soon as it had started, the snow lightened up and we went back inside.

We returned to our game of cards when I saw Daniel heading to the elevator. He wasn't far from me when I asked if he wanted to play cards with us. He said sure. We spent another hour playing cards before deciding to walk around the hotel.

It was like a museum turned hotel. We walked around upstairs, looking at all the intricate details that had gone into their ballrooms. People's photos hung on the wall. Random items like vases were on display. As our group spread out to explore the rooms, Daniel found me.

"Hey, you didn't have to invite me to hang out with you guys," he said.

"I know," I replied. I didn't know how else to respond.

He was silent as we walked through another room. "Thanks," he said.

I've always believed that people are worth giving second chances to. I'm not saying I was giving us another chance. But I did want him to know that I didn't have any hard feelings toward him. I had reservations, yes, but I knew that all the shit he had put me through wasn't personal. In fact, it was more about him externalizing the areas he needed to heal and I was the mirror at that time in his life. Every day is a new chance for you to grow and become your greatest version. It's hard to do that when people don't give you the chance to prove you have evolved. I was willing to give him the benefit of the doubt, and give him the space to show up as his best self.

Later in the trip, our group was offered a day trip to Niagara Falls. Your girl was definitely going. I was not going to miss a chance to go somewhere new. Once we were there, we walked along a gorgeous bridge that looped around the falls. It was snowing and I was stunned at how beautiful it was. I felt deeply at peace.

On our way to dinner, the bus driver pulled over for us to play in the snow. I think we all felt like kids again. It was magical. It was my favorite part of the trip, to be honest. Looking back at this memory, I think I might have taken it for granted a little bit. I hadn't done something that innocent and fun in a long time. Without noticing, I had forgotten what pure joy felt like until that moment. I had been more focused on school and grades and boys and whatever else I was into at the time. And I thought those things would bring joy. But joy is quiet and doesn't need to be found. Joy just is.

✳ ⵏ ⵏ ✳ ⵏ

One morning Daniel and I ended up hanging out around Buffalo. We got juice and talked about school and You-

Tube videos. I had missed talking with him. I had convinced myself that I would never find someone like that again... someone witty and smart, someone who could make me laugh. I wanted to take advantage of the small window we had to be "friends", even if it was only for a few days.

Most mornings involved us walking around getting breakfast or a juice. We never talked about our relationship and we never brought up anything heavy. Acting as friends felt like we were indirectly patching things up. We knew what we had both gone through. None of it had to be addressed. This trip was my opportunity to put my forgiveness into action. I wasn't bitter. I didn't hold the past against him. I allowed us to simply *be* while we were there. Buffalo forced me to release any expectations I would have normally had. He had a girl at home. I was taking the necessary steps to heal myself. I knew upfront this friendship was going to be repaired and remain in New York. And that was a relief.

One morning while waiting in line for breakfast, he had handed me his phone to look at something when his girl texted him. I don't know what it said, but her name had hearts beside it. I felt my face flush and gave him his phone saying, "Please take this back." I was embarrassed for being upset and stayed fairly silent the remainder of breakfast.

I don't think it's out of the ordinary to want to feel special when in a relationship. When in relationships, I wanted to know my significant others appreciated me and were happy being with me. I blame it on my love language being words of affirmation. I would notice every little thing the other person did for me. Whether it be texting me good morning or saving my name with hearts beside it, I wanted to experience the small things that showed they cared. I never got that reassurance from Daniel so to see him giving it to someone else was painful.

The best and worst part was it was not my business. It wouldn't have been beneficial for me to know why he put such little effort into our relationship. I had no right to know why because it wasn't actually about me. This is when I became aware that I was worth much more than the minimum amount I had gotten from him during our relationship. I was worthy of more than I imagined. But I had not taken the time to work through my limiting beliefs when it came to what I desired for myself. In turn, they kept popping up and I continued to humor them.

✳ ⋅⊹⋅ ✳ ⋅⊹⋅

The day before we left Buffalo, Daniel was suddenly standing in front of me. He leaned toward me as if to tell me something. I half-smiled, raising my eyebrows as if to say, "What's up?"

"Thanks for being nice to me."

I quietly stared at him for a few seconds and gently said, "I wasn't going to be mean to you."

"But you could have. So thanks," and he went on his way.

He was right. I could have ignored him the entire trip. I could have not gone out of my way to make him feel included. I could have hung out with my friends and not thought twice about him. It probably would have been easier for me. But

I didn't. I wanted to put my awareness and forgiveness into action rather than believing I had those traits with no evidence.

Buffalo was the big shift for me. I realized it was never going to work between me and Daniel. And I was perfectly okay with that. When I got back home, the rest of the semester breezed by. Summer was gentle with me. I remained focused on myself and what I wanted to get out of my last year in school. I spent most of my summer in my hometown. I was running every day at the local park. I was doing things for myself because I wanted to, not to prove anything to anyone. I wanted to feel the freedom I had kept myself from experiencing.

CHAPTER FOUR
The Tinder Age

When fall semester started back, Daniel had already graduated and moved out of state. This made everything easier on me. I got to focus on myself and my friends. I didn't have to be cautious with my emotions because I was surrounded by people I loved and trusted, who loved and respected me as well.

I felt it was time to put myself back out there. After all, 2013 was the beginning of the Tinder Age. The only thing easier to get than your roommate's Netflix password was a one-night stand.

So, I let myself go rogue. I had turned off my emotional connection with guys. I wanted to crunch three years' worth of dating experience into six months. I was doing what I wanted and didn't have to answer to anyone. I was doing this for the new me. I wanted to take back all the power I had given away. And the only way I thought I could achieve this was to sleep around.

College normally takes four years of your life. It's the time you're allowed to be wild and do as you please. For the first three and a half years, I felt as though I hadn't taken full advantage of the college experience. I had one semester and summer to make up for all the time I had wasted on one boy. For someone who was hell-bent on not letting these relationships get serious, I was desperately trying to cultivate connection.

Deep down, I did not believe that I would ever find a substantial relationship. I had so little self-respect and no recognition of my self-worth. This lack of self-love led me down a lonely path filled with horrible relationships, lies, disrespect, and shame. I was too terrified of healing. I hid behind unhealthy relationships and the idea that I wasn't good enough to have what I desired for myself. I put up with much more than I should have because on some level I thought I deserved it. More accurately, I thought I didn't deserve what I wanted for myself. This manifested instantly.

Rather than taking some much-needed time to heal myself, I continued to throw myself into relationship after relationship. I shushed my inner voice often enough that the voice of suffering took over my mind. I began believing the voice of suffering when it said I didn't deserve a healthy, loving relationship. I was stubborn and full of resentment. I thought that struggling in my relationships was going to make them turn out better. But relationships are not meant to be some emotional obstacle course. If it feels like that then the relationship may not be what is best for you.

There were many times where things would get better for a week but it never lasted. It was a vicious cycle of giving another chance, being proven wrong, and still giving another chance. I wish I could say this was exclusive to only one or two relationships but it wasn't. If I had respected and loved myself the way I desired to be by a partner, perhaps I would have ended those relationships sooner. But I was petrified of ending relationships, even when they were toxic. Back then, I thought being single was a defect. I thought my relationship status was the baseline for what I deserved in life. And if I didn't have a partner, then I was not worthy of anything.

I often second-guessed my intuition and dismissed my gut feelings. I didn't want to be alone. I didn't trust that there was someone better out there for me. I was more scared of being with myself than being in a bad relationship. I gave away my power by staying in relationships that were no longer good for me. I knew that if I was questioning whether what I was doing was for my highest good then I already knew the answer. But I often chose to ignore it.

My self-esteem was at an all-time low and it only got worse the more I dated. I didn't give myself an appropriate amount of time to heal, or figure out what I desired in a partner. I didn't love myself. I didn't know *how* to love myself. I thought investing in dating was going to build me back up. I believed that having a partner was the only way to be whole. I had no identity of my own so I clung to boys. I was insecure and too afraid to figure myself out. I set the bar depressingly low for myself and this was reflected in who I chose to date. I chose to date guys who needed a lot of healing so I could avoid working on myself. I put myself through a lot of self-imposed shit because I thought those were the rules. I thought I had to experience extreme lows before I could have a great relationship. And even then if I thought the guy was too good for me, I created the waves to make it true.

Take Kyle, for example. He and I had met at a mutual friend's birthday party. She introduced us and we clicked effortlessly. We exchanged numbers and went on a date a few weeks later when he came back to town.

I took him to a BBQ place where he finally broke the news to me that he was vegetarian. I was so embarrassed that I hadn't known but he was very understanding. We shared mac and cheese, collards, and cornbread. We ended up wandering around campus until 2 in the morning. On our way back to the car, he was in the middle of commenting on what he liked about me.

"You're sweet and nice," he said as he walked on the outside of the sidewalk.

A couple passed us and I said excuse me.

Kyle continued, "Very nice," and kind of chuckled.

It sounds backward considering my love language is words of affirmation, but I didn't know how to handle the compliments. I knew I was kind and nice, but it still felt strange to hear someone say they liked, well, *anything* about me. We got back to his car and he asked me if we could be official. Internally I was panicking. As much as I hoped for a boyfriend, this felt too easy. I was so surprised by his suggestion that I didn't even verbally answer. I only nodded.

I wasn't being honest with him. I didn't share the same feelings he was having. And I didn't want to lead such a good guy on. But here I was not being honest with what felt right for me in order to protect someone else's feelings. I was not in a place to date someone seriously. I had silenced my intuition by doing my own thing so often that this became second nature. I would have moments of internal guidance but fear always took me down a different route.

I got on Facebook within the next couple days to see Kyle had listed us "in a relationship" and I freaked out. I texted him immediately saying I thought it was too soon to become official. I had led him on because I was too afraid to communicate. I cared more about not hurting his feelings than being true to my own feelings.

This lesson was bound to get around to me sometime. I was rarely honest with myself about my feelings. I've always been great at feeling emotions but never actually expressing them. I suppressed my emotions because I thought they weren't important enough to be shared. I was also scared of how they would be received.

This carried over from childhood, from never having been encouraged to express how I actually felt. It also stemmed from my relationship with Daniel. I had been very communicative with him and it blew up in my face. My feelings weren't acknowledged, respected, or reciprocated. I decided that I would keep all my feelings inside. No one could disappoint me if I stayed arms-length away emotionally.

I convinced myself that approach was working, at least until Kyle. But I realized I was not respecting myself. I wasn't appreciating my own feelings because I was not expressing them. Suppressing my emotions became second nature. But it wasn't helping my personal growth. Slowly I began actively expressing my thoughts with the guys I dated. And by expressing them, I had to start with acknowledging my own emotions. It's been one of the most prominent healing experiences in my journey.

Working through our emotions is not supposed to be fun and enjoyable. It is supposed to help you heal. This is where the growth is. Don't put it off just because it's unpleasant. I had to heal a lot of emotional traumas before I found the strength to be vulnerable with my heart and emotions.

Kyle shifted my views on the guys I had been with and ultimately who I would date from that point on. No matter how much I believed my emotions weren't important, my partners deserved my honest feelings, just as I deserved to be honest with myself.

I found, through trial and error, that I created more genuine connections with the guys I dated when I was upfront about my feelings. Even though those relationships didn't work out, I learned a lot from them. I learned a lot about myself and what I wanted in a partner.

Unfortunately, I didn't put this into practice immediately. I stayed struggling with vocalizing my feelings because I was scared to get hurt. I didn't want to share my feelings and not have them recognized or reciprocated. The only way I felt emotionally safe was to maintain shallow relationships. So... no surprise: I jumped right back in the dating pool.

***

Dating has been redefined over the years. Dating apps are the new normal. The Netflix-and-Chill Era has peaked. People are afraid of catching feelings for fear that they would run the other person off or embarrass themselves. When I decided that I wanted to find a more meaningful relationship, I knew I would face a lot of hurdles.

I was in between my dating phase and my desire for a significant relationship. I knew myself well enough that I could easily backslide into the dating style I had been practicing. I was aware I would be met with resistance from the guys I would inevitably meet. I knew that if I tried again with any of the guys I had previously dated it would be difficult to start fresh with them. I didn't expect it to be easy. I was stepping out of the comfort zone I created to keep myself from getting hurt. But I was tired of playing it safe and keeping my heart hidden.

None of my past relationships were a waste of time. They taught me a lot even though with the majority of them I didn't learn the lesson until months or years later. They made me reevaluate what I desired in a partner. Not only that, they forced me to reflect on the woman I wanted to become. I recognized the pattern I was in: I entered into relationships because I was too afraid of being whole on my own. I deserved more than what I allowed myself to have.

Towards the end of 2015, I put most of my focus on bettering myself. I was shifting toward a plant-strong diet. I was introduced to spirituality. I was unlocking the door to the Universe inside myself. I was dabbling in the infinite glow of love I had kept locked away. It was terrifying but I was certain in my steps. I was finally sure of the direction I was headed.

After a few months of solitude, I decided to try again with

Kyle. This was another cycle I was trapped in. As soon as I saw any progress from working on myself, I would stop and throw that effort into another relationship. I was afraid of self-discovery. I was afraid of becoming whole on my own. I was worried I would not find fulfillment within myself. I thought it was impossible to find love if I was already complete on my own. I hid from my authentic and best self behind my romantic relationships.

Anyway, I had learned some new things about myself, which inspired me to give Kyle another shot. Once I saw how multifaceted I truly was, I wanted to get to know him with the same open-mindedness I had shown myself.

Kyle, being vegetarian when we met, was easy to talk to about my interest in plant-based eating. At that point in my life I was engulfed in environmental and health documentaries and articles. I felt a personal responsibility to the world to adopt this compassionate lifestyle. Luckily Kyle's experience as a vegetarian gave me the reassurance I needed to follow through with going plant-based. He was helpful and supportive while I was learning about this new lifestyle that I was adopting.

✳ ⊹ ✳ ⊹

I remember like it was yesterday. November 7, 2015. It was only 4 days before I turned 24. Kyle and I were headed to the Atlanta Vegetarian Food Festival. I didn't know it at the time but this event would change my entire life.

We stood in line, checking the list of all the vendors

who would be inside. We talked about which speakers we wanted to hear. We pet the stray cat that ended up going home with one of the sweet women in front of us. I felt so at ease around this group of people. We all shared a vision of a better, more compassionate and peaceful world. The best way I can describe it is that it was like I was meeting my tribe for the first time. I could feel it in the wind while in line, almost as if the Universe was saying, "Welcome home."

I was surrounded by people who shared my vision for this world. Everyone I met was kind, compassionate, open-minded, and hopeful. The VegFest opened me up to a whole new world that I didn't know existed. And I was running toward it with open arms.

Soon after the VegFest, Kyle and I amicably went our separate ways. Our relationship was over, but what I'd started investigating while I was with him was going to take me much further.

CHAPTER FIVE
A New Relationship

The University of Georgia has a lovely tradition once someone graduates. The Arch is an iron structure located downtown that connects to the campus. When I was there for freshman orientation, all of the orientation leaders told us how it was bad luck to walk underneath The Arch before you graduated. They told us new kids about the tradition of walking under The Arch only after you graduated, signifying walking into a new chapter of life. It was at that moment I heard a small voice inside of me say, *Yeahhh, we're not going to be doing that.*

The voice was not demeaning. Its tone was not that of someone smugly telling me I was incapable of graduating. Instead it was compassionate and playful, almost hinting that there was more on the horizon for me than I could imagine. It was like my intuition had been planning a surprise party over the last decade. Sure, she was allowing me to drive. But throughout the trip she continually suggested that I actually had no idea what was going on; that I would be totally surprised with the destination.

While at university, I switched between being a Linguistics

major to a French major to a Public Relations major for a few weeks, to an Early Childhood Education major for a semester, and then finally back to a French major. I was all over the place. I loved learning but I did not enjoy going to school. I hated class. I threw up in my mouth every time I had to write papers on things that did not interest me. I would draw and redraw blueprints for how I thought my life was supposed to look after college but they were never quite right. Something always felt off with the vision I carried as "my own". And I realized it was because that was never my vision. It was never what I wanted for myself.

As I struggled with figuring out what I was meant to do, I remained in school for four years out of obligation. I was smart and capable. I could have easily finished up and gotten my degree. But I had no interest. Which I think is the hardest thing about dropping out of school. People expect you to have some grand reason like, "I created this app that's going to revolutionize social media!" or "I'm pregnant with triplets!" or "I won the lottery so I don't have to work for the rest of my life!"

I did not have one of these concrete reasons that carried physical evidence proving I could make it without a degree. I did not have a reason that would resonate with those prodding me about when I would go back to get my degree. Any answer I gave was not logical in their eyes.

I would not have been able to explain it at the time but deep down I knew that I was on a path created *for* me and not *by* me. If I had kept down that lane of doing what was expected of me, I don't think I would have discovered my life's purpose. I doubt I would be writing this book.

The freedom I found at university was life altering. I relished the ability to choose what I did and did not do. I savored the power I had to govern myself. It was liberating and gratifying being in control of my path. I'm not saying all my choices were winners but I loved the independence I had. It didn't just give me space to spread my wings. It allowed me the opportunity to reevaluate my dreams and discover myself. And I wanted to carry that feeling with me for the rest of my life. I knew there was a different path for me and I needed to honor it. The only person I had to justify my decision to was myself.

So midway through my final year of college, I did it: I dropped out of school.

✳ ❄ ✳

Quitting school. Quitting meat. Quitting Kyle. In a short amount of time, my life was changing a lot. With New Year's 2016 around the corner, I felt like it was the perfect time to start some momentous life changes.

I researched everything I could about veganism and sustainable living. I knew this was a shift I wanted to embrace. One of my New Year's Resolutions for 2016 was to become fully vegan by the end of the year. I knew myself well enough that if I tried to dive right into veganism, I wouldn't stick with it. Everyone is different in their approach to a new chapter. It was important for me to listen to my intuition. I wanted to be successful when it came to my goals for the New Year.

Another resolution I had: no sex outside of a relationship. I wanted a substantial relationship before being intimate again. This was a big resolution for me to stick with. I didn't like dating around because I didn't like who I was when I did that. I knew I could be a better me. I was building back up my inner confidence on my own. I've always identified myself with whomever I was seeing, so this was going to be a major task. I had been hiding behind boys for years. I didn't know who I was. I was scared that when I discovered my best self, I might run away from her, just as I had run away from self-love. I worried that the people around me wouldn't like her. I didn't know how to discover who I was. But all that mattered was I was willing to be vulnerable and find her.

✳︎⁑⟟⁑⟟⁑

The beginning of 2016 started out gentle and encouraging. I felt my inner self shifting and healing those parts of me I was ashamed of. This occurred through seven keys: meditation, a plant-based lifestyle, saying "no" to casual sex, radical self-love, cultivating intuition, spirituality, and exercise.

✳︎⁑⟟⁑⟟⁑

Meditation

I cannot speak highly enough about beginning a meditation practice, even if it is only for 20 minutes a day. Meditation is what held my hand down this path of becoming my greatest version. I started out with guided meditations, simply because I couldn't stay focused for long when I tried to meditate on my own.

Meditation unlocked all the doors inside of me that I had boarded up. It even introduced me to doors I didn't know I had. I was able to find answers in the silence. I was learning about myself without having to be loud about it. Meditation led me back to my inner child and my highest self.

Meditation helped me more than I can put into words. The one piece of advice I have for anyone is to start meditating. Whether you struggle with love, anger issues, stress, or want to learn something new, meditation has infinite benefits. With regular practice, meditation can feel like flipping a light switch. After meditating consistently, I found my world was a lot simpler than my mind had previously made it out to be. Meditation allowed me to create space between myself and my thoughts. Instead of always thinking and overanalyzing, I was surprised when one day I realized I wasn't attaching myself to my thoughts. I felt as though I could see my thoughts going across my mind like movie credits. With this detachment from my thoughts, I found much more peace than I thought was possible.

Meditation also helped me to open up to myself. This was hard for me, which explains why I struggled immensely with opening up to partners; as within, so without. I hesitated revealing all of me to myself. And holding onto that fear, I couldn't genuinely expect myself to open up fully to another person. During my meditation sessions, I discovered a lot of childhood traumas that I carried into my adult relationships. My confidence as a child was never built up. I was hypersensitive to other people's opinions about me. I never felt like being myself was enough for the people around me. And the people I looked up to didn't think they were enough either.

The more research I did about meditation, the more I learned about its power to lower stress. Meditation continued to create a gap between seeing what was going on around me and how I responded to it, if I decided to. I found anything outside of me only has power if I respond to it. If I didn't have a reaction, would the outside situation leave me feeling the same? Of course not. And if I feel overwhelmed, I say to myself, "I'm choosing to be in this moment." This helps me center back into my power.

One night, I was pulling out of my neighborhood and almost T-boned this truck. It was my fault. I hadn't looked left and started to pull out before slamming on my brakes. I expected him to flip me off, or glare at me. But he didn't. He just kept on driving. He didn't even look over at me. And I thought to myself, *Damn, I want to be that calm!* I think of him every time I start to get annoyed with drivers, or people in general. This awareness allows me to start seeing things happen in front of me rather than feeling like I am going through them. I am pulled back into awareness rather than remaining in my head. My open door to return to the present moment is when I catch myself lost in thoughts.

A Plant Based Lifestyle

Being meat-free also helped tremendously to start off my self-love journey. Cutting out meat from my diet altered my state of mind immensely. I was no longer eating dead animals and that in and of itself was uplifting. I wasn't consuming the sadness, grief, and fear those animals had in their last moments. I also felt my karmic cycle release. I had been the person who would not squish a bug, citing karma, but would still eat a hamburger. I was finally aligning my thoughts with action. I was, in small steps, trying to create a more peaceful world by practicing a compassionate lifestyle.

No More Casual Sex

Then there was my choice not to have sex outside a relationship. I wasn't consuming a man's energy either. I think this is an important topic that doesn't get discussed enough, not only for women but also men. Do you trust your partner? Do they trust you? Have you had the hard conversations about the emotional and mental aspects that come from being physical with each other? How would you feel if you or your partner got pregnant?

I first learned about sex when I was in middle school. All the girls were put in one room, the boys in another. We were taught the physical aspects of sex. We were told exactly how babies are made. They told us about how to have safe sex, referring to condoms, birth control, and abstinence.

It wasn't until I was 24 that I understood there were two more aspects to sex that are rarely, if ever, mentioned: mental and emotional. We are taught about how to be preventative when it comes to pregnancy and STDs. We are given ways to protect our physical body during sex, but not our spiritual body. It's rare to be taught how to protect your mental and emotional spaces when they relate to sex.

In society today, sex is excessively recreational. Speaking for myself, I blame it on the removal of emotional intimacy from sex. I remember justifying my Tinder Age by saying, "I've turned off my emotions." It was the farthest thing from the truth. I was too busy suppressing my emotions to take the time to figure out what was healthiest for me.

Casual sex was not healthy for me. Society sees sex as something that should only benefit us physically. For example, have you ever heard of the Sex Diet? It's a weight loss plan that replaces normal exercise with sex. I mean…nothing inherently wrong with that; you do you, honey. But I think sex should be seen as something more sacred.

I'm not saying the only way sex can be special is by waiting until your wedding night. But what is wrong with allowing sex to become special again? Is it our collective fear of intimacy? What about our eye-widening fear of vulnerability? Or is it perhaps we are too lazy to want anything more than a physical pick-me-up? The sex health talk needs to be extended beyond the physical to include emotional and mental health. For me, casual sex led to higher anxiety, lower self-esteem, loneliness, and depression.

I was only aware of physical protection but not emotional and mental protection. I didn't have the knowledge or the tools to protect my spiritual self when it came to sex. I didn't like myself and yet I thought sex was the only way I could heal myself. But sex kept making it worse. I put my emotional and mental health in the other person's hands, hoping they would have the Midas touch that would fix me. I didn't know that all along I was the only one that could both protect and heal myself.

When I decided to stop having casual sex, it was the first time I felt empowered. This was when I could feel my spirit being built back up. I needed to stop loving myself part-time and instead make it my top priority. The more time I spent loving myself rather than loving on someone else, I realized, "This is how I become whole."

Society is so sex driven that we have forgotten how to establish real connections without being physical. Casual sex has become as common and unhealthy as a fast food place; a cheap fix that leaves you wanting more. It's easy to focus on the physical aspect of sex rather than the emotional or mental aspects. A person can easily hide behind sex to protect their ego. I did for a long time. I was terrified of getting to know myself and loving myself so I threw all my energy into guys. Only when I removed sex did I realize I had been hiding behind it. And I found I wanted sex to be precious. Once my perception of sex changed, even more healing took place.

My view on sex has shifted drastically. I have redefined what sex means to me. I am no longer giving away parts of myself; I am always whole. I know what I bring to the table. I know my worth. I used to think this was a distasteful part of my journey but it has been pivotal in leading me towards my best self. Without my old self, I wouldn't have gotten here. And this is the most important work I have ever done.

Radical Self Love

I reeled back all my sexual energy and transmuted it into loving myself. By monogamously dating myself, I cultivated the space to put myself first. I remember one night I was at my kitchen table thinking, *I can't wait to be with a man that will make me a cup of tea after I've had a rough day.* Or: *I would adore being with a man who will make me a cup of coffee exactly how I like it simply because he is giving.* Suddenly, I realized I was sitting there not holding myself to the same standard I was holding my future partner. Even when I needed a cup of tea, I wouldn't make myself one. This was the spark I needed to begin intentionally dating myself. It sounds cliché, dating yourself, but it was the best first step I took toward healing my heart.

Dating myself involves me setting aside time to decompress from my day exactly how I would with a partner. In the past, I didn't enjoy spending time with myself. I would search for partners that I could throw all my energy into rather than continuing healing myself. This is when I had the Cup of Tea Revelation. Ever since then, I intentionally set aside time to do things for myself that I would love to do for a partner, and also that I would appreciate a partner doing for me. I have little date nights with myself and take myself out for breakfast. I do things for myself that I would still do if I had a partner. I had to start treating myself as a whole, rather than sit at home feeling like a half. The more intentionally I put effort into myself, the more effort I can put into a future partner.

It sounds contradictory. How can I have any effort left to give if I'm putting all of my efforts into self-love and healing? But when you fill your cup to the brim, and it's overflowing, it becomes effortless to give back to a partner. You wouldn't be pulling the effort from your reserves. The effort and love are spilling over into your partner from what you have already invested in yourself. The love you give yourself is going to reflect out and come back to you.

So...making myself a cup of tea while listening to my record player and journaling about how my day went might sound trivial but it has altered how deeply I love myself. It made me realize how worthy I am of what I desire for myself.

When I was younger, I was consistently told that boys wouldn't like me because I was a tomboy and a bigger girl. I was told I should dress nicer, paint my nails, and do my hair so guys would like me. Don't get me wrong; I wanted boys to like me. But when I was told *I* needed to change to be more desired, I felt like who I was would never be good enough.

The older I got, the more I juggled between being authentic and adjusting myself depending on whoever I was interested in. There is still a cultural expectation today that women need to be a certain way and do certain things to attract and keep a man but bleep that. There is someone out there who is going to love every part of you. Dimming your light will not help you find them.

What you hear growing up will deeply affect the quality of your inner voice. I was surrounded by people who spoke poorly to themselves. Self-deprecation was expected. God forbid anyone talk about what they loved about themselves. I had no example of what it looked like to truly love who you are. This spilled over into adulthood. All of this was embedded in my voice of suffering. I wasn't aware I was carrying around these traumas and I hadn't been taught how to fix them.

My journey required me to love myself first before I could even entertain the idea of finding love. I was frustrated that I had to love myself before I could expect someone else to properly love me. I thought external love was indicative of how much I was allowed to love myself. But external love will never compensate for a lack of self-love. No one told me that finding love was a two-part process. I felt defenseless and insecure when I realized I had no baseline for love in my life. I was embarrassed by the space I took up. I didn't enjoy my own company. In general, I didn't like myself. And if I didn't like myself, I was quite far from loving myself.

I discovered that self-love is the baseline for how much love I find in my life. I could not expect to find love in the world until I had found love within myself. I trusted this process and took as much time as I needed to get where I am today. But this evolution to radical self-love and acceptance has no end because evolution is not the goal. The goal is to know yourself completely, and to love and accept yourself as you are. Growth will be a natural byproduct of self-awareness and self-discovery. I will continue learning, growing, and healing for as long as I am here. And that is beautiful.

There are many reasons why people struggle with love.

My struggle stemmed from not knowing how to love myself properly. Since I was a kid, I have been told what is "good" and "bad" about me. These outside opinions had a big impact on how I treated myself. I took other people's opinions of me and placed them above the opinion I had of myself. And I eventually adopted those beliefs as my own. Then instead of trying to discover if those opinions were in fact what I truly thought about myself, I just went on believing them. I unconditionally trusted everyone except myself. I had more faith and trust in other people's opinions about me than I did my own. When I stopped doing the small things, like trusting my gut, I eventually stopped doing the big things too, like loving myself.

I was always under the impression that loving yourself unconditionally made you selfish, conceited, detached, cocky, proud...you get the idea. People put themselves on hold because somehow that's been portrayed as humble or heroic, but it's not. It's a tragedy. Folks live their lives based on other people's expectations of them and wonder why they're unhappy. We're told all this energy and love is supposed to be given away. And in some respects, it is. You know that saying "whatever you give you will get back tenfold"? That same logic applies when you do that for yourself. When you intentionally put yourself first, the energy behind it will continue manifesting. The beautiful thing about this is it happens instantly.

This was a process. I didn't all of a sudden love every aspect of myself. I was patient with myself. I gave myself the space to succeed at my own pace. I knew I could love myself completely; I just needed to allow myself to do so. This is how I thought about it: imagine putting extra energy and effort into your romantic partner. Often when we do this, we've put out an expectant energy. We wait to receive the same (or more) from that person. We give them the power to make us feel fulfilled or not by depending on what they give us in return. But when you serve yourself like a king or queen, that energy is immediately felt and received by your soul. There's no waiting game when it comes to the benefits of self-love. The more consistently you practice self-love, the less awkward you will feel for putting yourself first. And most importantly, the easier it will be to master radical self-acceptance.

Love is the key, but self-love is the master key. Self-love sets the tone for the love you experience in life. That love is mirrored outwardly, naturally radiant without force; and then it's reflected back to you. I am not here to preach about how self-love is the root of all love. I am here to share with you how rediscovering the love I had hidden from myself helped me create a life that is more brilliant than I could have ever dreamed.

Here is an exercise that I did a lot during my journey to self-love. I want you to objectively look at how much you love yourself. This includes physically, mentally, emotionally… all of it. Be honest with where you are at this moment. Do not feel ashamed or scared. Now write down your positive attributes. Everything you love or enjoy about who you are, write it down.

Do you have your list? Write a couple more things down. At this point you should be having a hard time stopping.

That's the goal. You should feel the snowball effect of how good it feels to express what you love about yourself. Okay, the positive attribute list is complete. Now I want you to write down what you perceive to be your negative attributes. Once done, I want you to take a look at the list of negative things you've written about yourself. I need you to determine why you categorize those things as negative. Who told you that those things are "bad"? I guarantee that the stigma behind those "negative" attributes did not come from inside of you.

Judging yourself is not natural and yet we have been conditioned to do so from an early age. An outside source told you that those things were bad. An outside source told you that it's bad to speak your mind, it's bad that you have a smart mouth, and it's bad to eat ice cream for breakfast. They told you that it's bad to love yourself. They made you feel like it's poor taste to shine brightly. They told you it's bad to quit the job you hate because "at least you have insurance." They told you it's too risky to do what you want and follow your heart.

Outside sources will tell anything to make you feel smaller than you are destined to be. Outside sources will never give you a clear image of yourself. But they have no jurisdiction in telling you what is right for you because they are not you. This list of "negative" attributes isn't negative at all because negativity is all relative. It's similar to that quote, "The beauty is in the eye of the beholder." Well, I believe that negativity is in the eye of the beholder.

Opinions are constant and they can stick with you. You hear that it's not normal to love yourself or that it's conceited to think you're beautiful. All of these opinions are other people telling you what they believe to be "bad". That is *their* reality. Do not let their reality invade yours. Don't let it alter the reality you have of yourself. Don't allow someone else to govern how you feel about yourself, how you feel about your decisions, or how you feel about following your heart and your truth. No one else can tell you what is right for you except *you*.

Don't let someone else's struggles become your struggles. Everyone is struggling with something different. It's easy for people to project their challenges onto other people so they aren't the only one going through them. Absorbing other people's projections and insecurities can easily make them seem like they are your own. At the same time, we need to be conscientious of projecting our struggles onto other people. The most frequent example is when we complain.

Complaining has become one of the biggest addictions in society. It's free. It's got no obvious physical side effects. And practically everyone is doing it. Complaining has almost become an expectation, like when you go to dinner with a friend who just wants to talk negatively about people. And yes, it's easy to complain. Complaining is the accepted form of our voice of suffering. We want everyone to listen. But the energy behind that voice of suffering is easily transferred, intentionally or not.

If you find you are the one who always has something negative to say, this is your opportunity to heal whatever hurt is still inside of you. Why are you angry with your partner? Why are you complaining about your roommate? Why are you pissed at your coworker? Why are you jealous that your friend got a promotion? Why are you allowing all of this toxic energy to invade your sacred space?

It's because pity parties are free. It is easier to sit there, play the victim, and complain rather than look within to figure out how to heal the pain that is surfacing. Everyone gets annoyed, angry, judgmental, or whichever emotion your voice of suffering chooses to speak through. However your voice of suffering prefers to emote, you can teach yourself to become unattached to these thoughts. When you catch yourself being consumed by that emotion, the most important step is to become aware that you are having them. Then you can begin witnessing these thoughts without attachment, allergy, or reluctance.

When we get swept up in emotions that don't serve us, such as anger or fear, our body responds with stress hormones. When I complain, I find the same stress symptoms as when I'm angry or judgmental. Fuming over a problem will cause the body to constantly supply more of the stress hormone cortisol. High levels of cortisol are linked to depression, lower immune function, heart disease, high blood pressure, and lower life expectancy.

Okay, let me blind you with science for just a moment. I'm not a doctor. I dropped out of college, remember? But I've learned a lot these past two years and I want to share it with you.

Did you know 80% of serotonin is created in your gut? What you eat literally has the power to change the chemistry in your brain. When I started eating plant-based, I found eating intuitively truly allowed me to feed my body what it needed rather than what my taste buds wanted. I had to ask myself if the foods I ate were healing me or harming me.

Neural pathways begin to harden in the brain by the time we are 25. At this moment, I'm only 26 years old which means how I have spoken to myself over the course of my entire life has started to harden in my brain. It's like if you take the same route to work for 40 years; that path is embedded in your mind. You don't even have to think about how you are going to get to work. Your thoughts are the route you take to work. Do you take the route with all the potholes that you are used to, even though it damages your car? Or are you willing to try a different route, one that will be gentler and less abrasive but is out of your comfort zone?

When we become aware of our thoughts, we can rewire these pathways to create new ones, which will increase activity in the brain. No matter how old you are, now is always the time to reflect on how you have spoken to yourself over the course of your lifetime. Has the voice of suffering taken up residence in your mind? Mindfulness makes this conscious reprogramming of your mind effortless. We can consciously monitor our thoughts, feel our emotions, and focus our attention. The more intentionally we practice these things, the easier it becomes to deepen the awareness of your mind. These practices will help create new neural pathways to avoid the voice of suffering and ultimately lead you to having a peaceful and positive mind.

As I began to unravel my own mysteries and actively work on myself, I found I liked the woman I was discovering. For as long as I can remember, I had been told to be this or that;

to shrink myself in order for other people to feel comfortable around me. And the price of being comfortable around others but feeling uncomfortable with myself was not worth it anymore. I stopped allowing myself to be attached to people's opinions of me. Instead of putting my focus and energy there, I began listening for my inner voice. I wanted to strengthen my intuition and be on the same team again.

Cultivating Intuition

I view intuition as a muscle. The more we listen to our inner guidance, the more clearly we can hear it over time. You know how sometimes you'll ask yourself a question and without effort, you'll receive an answer? That's intuition. Intuition allows us to feel a freedom while living our truth without caring what anybody thinks. It's not about one person being right and the other being wrong. Being in alignment with your highest self is liberating. You are allowed to be unaffected by other people's words and actions. You are allowed to be free from other people's opinions of you. You have the freedom to live without requiring a response from others. You can allow everything to *be* without adding an adjective to it. And that's what intuition gave me: freedom to follow my heart.

Now there is a difference between intuition and fear, even if they come across in a similar manner. Fear makes you feel you need to do something immediately. If your gut reaction feels more like fight or flight, that's fear. Intuition doesn't make you feel rushed to make a decision, but rather excited to move forward. Intuition is gentle in guiding you to do what is best for you. Intuition is like a spiritual chiropractor trying to get you back into alignment.

And we are constantly on a learning curve. Every single day is a learning opportunity. Instead of looking months or years ahead, I try to take each day at a time and hear what my mind and body are telling me the lesson is. I believe my highest self communicates with me as my intuition.

I was speaking with a friend recently and I said, "I think my highest self has gotten louder."

My friend's response was, "I don't think she's getting louder. I think your ears are just clearing up." And it was true. The more I trusted my intuition, the more clearly I heard it. And the more clearly I heard it, the more I listened for it. It was a snowball effect. I would ask questions and listen for answers. I'd ask for signs and trust what showed up. But I'm not perfect. There were times when I desired to control situations so much that I wouldn't trust what showed up. I would continue to ask for signs. I could feel my highest self get annoyed and I would hear very clearly, "Stop asking! Just trust me!"

I began living a life rooted in compassion not only for animals and the planet but also for myself. I was finally treating myself with respect. I began every day by speaking kindly to myself. I was rediscovering my worth as each day went by. I could feel my soul illuminating as I grew and began to trust myself more and more.

Spiritual Awakening

In the first few months of 2016, I was also reintroduced to spirituality. I grew up in church, so I wasn't unfamiliar with the idea of being spiritual. But my experience of church was not great. I found it to be a place that thrived off greed, judgment, and division. I would hear people around me saying others were going to hell for multitudes of reasons. It never made sense to me. If the Universe, or God, or Source, however you choose to call the Divine, created you exactly how you were supposed to be then there was no way you were going to be punished for living your truth. I didn't want to be associated with any group that clung to animosity and ostracism. Once I removed myself from a fear-based environment that encouraged separation, hate, and judgment, I found a world that craved authenticity, compassion, and love.

After starting a consistent meditation practice I found I hadn't been respecting the Universe because I didn't respect who I was. It was no wonder I believed the Universe had abandoned me. I had abandoned myself. I had lost my sense of purpose, felt worthless, and didn't feel loved. But when I began intentionally loving myself, I was able to see that the Universe had my back the entire time. The Universe could only give me what I was already giving myself. The Universe taught me that everything is mirrored from what is already inside you.

By reconnecting with the Universe, I began tapping into the light inside of me. I acknowledged the force I had inside myself and started to actively and intentionally respect it. By allowing myself to be vulnerable and opening myself up to spirituality, I was reintroduced to my highest self. I was finally able to see the thread of connection between me and everyone around me. Meditation allowed me to drop into this space of oneness with the world. My heart opened up in a way I never thought it would, or could. I found my misplaced worth and self-love. My self-healing was an act of resistance to every outdated narrative I'd had throughout my life. And in this space I remembered who I am.

In early 2016, I was also introduced to the Law of Attraction. I was scrolling through YouTube looking for my next guided meditation and found one that was specifically for manifesting. The Law of Attraction is the belief that whatever you focus on, whether positive or negative, will manifest into your life accordingly. When I first researched it, I thought it sounded like magic, or at least something made up. But I remained open-minded, as I had been with veganism and meditation.

The more I learned about the Law of Attraction and manifesting, I found that I had to set the baseline for anything I hoped to have in my life. If I wanted love, I had to love myself 100%. If I wanted to be financially stable, I had to believe I was worthy of abundance.

Let me interject and say that abundance is not synonymous with money. You can be abundant in love, time, finances, opportunities, and practically anything else. Abundance is always available and never lacking. Only when I started cherishing what I was bountiful in did I find more to be grateful for.

I had to be explicit with my intentions and trust the Universe would deliver what I needed. I quickly realized that what I had been putting out—pun intended—was what I was getting back. I was putting out desperation, shame, and disrespect. The vibes I gave off were determining my physical reality.

Imagine reality as a literal mirror. In the mirror, you can't frown and expect your reflection to smile. You can't force your mirrored self to smile when you aren't first smiling. And when you smile, the mirror has no choice but to smile back because the mirror, like reality, has no mind of its own. Your mind creates your reality. In the past, I would repeatedly say that my love life sucked. And the Universe had no choice but to give me what I believed to be true. Each person has the power to create the life they want. Reality has no choice but to respond accordingly.

People give and receive energy much like banks give out and receive money. Imagine your bank having two main components: fluid energy, which can be given to and received from external sources, and energy reserves, which are only to be used on ourselves. The reason issues arise surrounding our energy bank is that we loan out our reserves to other people. When you put more effort into someone else and don't replenish yourself, that's when you feel drained, unloved, anxious, depressed, and even unworthy.

You are in charge of the bank. You have the divine right

to vet people before loaning out your energy. And if some-one overdrafts your energy: "RED FLAG — This account has been frozen and pending action will result in an immediate closing of this account. No thanks for doing business with us. BYEEEE!" Close the accounts and dismiss the people that are no longer good for you. You are the curator of your inner circle.

We must remember to take care of ourselves first. It is not selfish to love yourself. It is not horrible to cut people off who only take. It is not conceited to take care of yourself and give yourself what you need. It's honorable and respectable. It will inspire the people around you to love themselves so hard that they rediscover their light and their worth.

A New Exercise Paradigm

It's incredible to me the unhealthy relationship I used to have with exercise. I was the slowest runner on my sports teams. I was always self-conscious about my weight and how less-than I felt while playing sports. Gym class was a nightmare. Exercise felt like torture to me. I grew up thinking exercise was only for physical health. I only ever focused on exercise when I wanted to lose weight.

This narrative followed me into 2016. I was making a lot of progress in different areas of my life so I decided to join a gym. I went to the gym several times a week, oftentimes driving my ass there while complaining that I didn't want to go. And once I arrived I would think, *Well, I'm here now so I might as well get a workout in.* My only goal in the gym was to lose weight. Funnily enough, the more I focused on losing weight, the less weight I lost and the more I slipped back into the unhealthy state of mind I had previously been in.

I hate to admit it but one of the reasons I joined the gym was because of my New Year's Resolution not to sleep with anyone outside of a relationship. I thought by being over-weight that I was unworthy of a relationship. In my mind, I was going to get in shape and my future partner would just appear. I thought exercise was going to help me achieve all that I desired for myself. And while it took another year to create a healthy relationship with exercise, I learned a lot in those few months I dedicated myself to the gym.

I learned that my motivation to succeed has to be pure and not just to achieve something externally, like a relationship. I learned that exercise is not the master key to my happiness. I learned that I am always exactly where I am supposed to be. I learned that the body recognizes anxiety and excitement as the same thing, physiologically. It's the mind that creates the positive or negative attachment. So instead of dreading going to the gym, I started saying, "I'm excited!" It's all about the mindset, baby. And I learned that I can never outrun my lessons no matter how in shape I am. My struggle with self-worth was not going to heal just by losing weight. I had to learn how to be preventative and proactive in protecting my health. I was tired of benching myself when it came to taking control of my life. I was tired of feeling lethargic and bitter. I was ready to hold myself accountable for my healing. I gave myself permission to be my best version because I am worthy.

The wisdom from these lessons have never left me. In 2017, when I dedicated myself to radical self-transformation, I hired a life coach. I thought he might tell me to go to the gym twice a day or something unbearable like that. But he didn't. Instead he asked me to walk just one mile a day, as slowly as I liked. After doing that for a week, I began enjoying my walks. One mile eventually turned into five; the walking turned into running. Without even knowing it, I began seeing exercise as something that benefits my mind rather than a tool for losing weight. That slight shift in how I approached my exercise regimen completely altered how I moved forward in my relationship with exercise. As I transformed my mind, the transformation of my body followed. Walking became a movement-mediation. For the first month, I didn't even weigh myself. I didn't look at walking as a physical exercise as it had become so much more to me.

Changing your perception changes the chemistry in your body. Everything done with intention is changing yourself and the vibration of this planet. And this change in perception toward exercise transformed me. When I stopped pressuring myself to heal my body and chose to focus on healing as a whole, with my mental and spiritual health at the forefront, the positive effects in my body soon followed.

CHAPTER SIX

Attaching, Then Abstaining

Something came over me in March 2016. I was talking with my two best friends and expressed to them that I wanted to download Tinder again. I don't know if I was bored, or if my gut was telling me I would meet someone on there, but I downloaded it. Low and behold, I met a boy. My tagline on Tinder read, "What was the last book you read?" and he responded with the name of a vegan cookbook that I had recently bought. It felt like fate.

His name was Justin. For one of our first dates, we went hiking. He was patient with me as I stopped every ten minutes to take a picture. When we reached the top he asked if we could take a picture. It was the first time a guy had asked me to take a picture with him on a date. It was sweet and flattering. Then we kissed. It was the most romantic place I had ever had a first kiss. But I didn't feel anything. There was no spark; no internal voice yelling, "YES, GIRL, HE'S IT! HE'S THE ONE!" There was no explanation for why I didn't feel it. I just didn't.

We headed back to get my car when he told me he wanted to make us official. I was immediately taken back to when Kyle had asked me in his car to be official. But unlike with Kyle, I wanted to be with Justin. I had evolved since dating Kyle. And Justin had a lot of qualities I wanted in a partner. He seemed sweet and patient. He was a vegan. It didn't hurt that he was hot as hell. So I said yes.

*⁎⎯⁑⁖⁑⁖

The more Justin and I got to know each other, the more little red flags would pop up that I ignored. I was selectively colorblind back then. The first sight of a red flag, and I would go red-blind. All I saw was green, so I said to myself, "Whelp, it's green now so I guess I'll just go, go, go! There is no such thing as red!"

Justin had the few qualities that were non-negotiable at that time in my journey so I figured I could deal with some discord. But there was a larger percentage of qualities I did not find inviting.

The first example I can think of should have concerned me more at the time. We were talking about past relationships and he disclosed to me that some of his previous partners had told him he was controlling. "Do you think I'm controlling?" he asked me. I told him I didn't think so. But in truth, I didn't know him well enough to determine whether he was controlling or not. I remember thinking it was strange for him to ask me that, having only known each other for a couple weeks. But from my experience, whenever a guy asked me questions that required me to negate what one of their previous partners had told them, there was usually a lot of truth to what those partners had said.

Justin needed constant reassurance, which I was happy to give him. But I ended up putting more effort into making him feel comfortable in the relationship than I was putting into myself. He made me feel as though I needed to stop putting myself first. It was as if he was uncomfortable with me knowing my worth.

The first couple months of the relationship were rocky. I was looking for a new job, and I confided in him a lot about the stress I felt concerning my career. He told me he thought I wasn't as positive as I had led him to believe I was. I didn't know how to defend myself. I wanted my partner to listen to me as I listened to him. But whenever something got difficult or required us to talk something out, he did not want to engage in the conversation. I don't know why I tried so hard to convince him to be patient with me, but I did.

I'm quite fond of my alone time. I'm an introvert and self-reliant. But Justin didn't like being apart from me. Whenever we were in separate places, he would flood my phone with text messages. I felt smothered.

I disclosed my romantic history to him and he did not like it. His reaction made me uncomfortable but I still wanted to be honest. I prided myself on being truthful with him the entire relationship and many times, he did not like what I had to say.

He wanted me to feel bad about my entire dating history to build himself up. And I wasn't going to do that. I explained to him that not feeling guilty doesn't mean that I'm proud of it. It was not my responsibility to make him feel comfortable and secure with my past. I had accepted it, and if he couldn't then it was not going to work between us. I wasn't going to live in the past, and I wasn't going to dredge it up every time he wanted to make me feel lesser than him.

✳ ⊹ ✳ ⊹

In June, the best thing happened. I dropped my phone in the toilet. It gave me a much-needed break from my overbearing boyfriend. He required an excessive amount of attention and I consistently felt exhausted. Between me and you, some days I would purposefully leave my phone at home so I could get some peace and quiet. He required constant attention and validation, which left little time for me to spend with myself.

After my phone fell in the toilet, I went a week without a phone. Justin and I were chatting on Facebook and I told him I wanted to run to a couple stores. He was being lazy in deciding whether or not he would come over, and I got tired of waiting for him. I told him I was leaving.

I got to the store, and as I was perusing the aisles, Justin came up behind me. He said he had been planning to come over to my house so we could drive together. But I hadn't waited on him. I was doing something for myself. I was drained from having to back up my decisions because he was too insecure to let me out of his sight.

When we got to my car, I showed him the shirt I had almost worn. It was a spaghetti strap shirt, perfect for summertime.

He said, "I'm glad you didn't wear that. It's kind of revealing…"

Cue eye roll. He was skilled at making me second-guess myself and my decisions, even the ones I had made before I met him. I could feel my self-love shrinking back. Instead of filling my own cup, I was giving Justin all the power. I was struggling with being true to myself and worrying about what my boyfriend thought about me.

In my previous relationships, my self-esteem was quite low. I was always too embarrassed to ask where things were going. And even when I did, I rarely believed whatever they told me. If they said they only wanted sex, I convinced myself they were scared of being vulnerable, so I tried harder to make it work long term. If they told me they wanted a relationship, I pulled back to see if they were being honest. I always wanted someone who would be communicative and honest with me. Yet I was never honest with myself first. I always wanted to know how the other person felt before figuring out how I felt. I was pulled back into an outdated cycle of trusting another person's feelings before my own.

※ ⫶⫶ ※ ⫶⫶

Justin and I disagreed on a lot of things. The most prominent disagreements revolved around women's rights. He tensed up at the idea that women were allowed to feel free and comfortable in their skin. He was not supportive of the thought that women could do what they wanted. In our relationship, he was not fond of the fact that I did not feel the need to ask his permission to do anything. There was one time I had put on some shorts, getting ready to go to the store. He looked at me and said, "Are you wearing those?"

"Yeah, I'm going to the store."

"I would not respect a woman who wore those."

All I heard was: *Emma, I don't respect you, no matter how much you respect yourself.*

I wasn't allowed to wear shorts during the summer but he was allowed to post shirtless photos on Instagram? I was dating someone who told me he loved me but it was always conditional on whether or not he approved of my actions. He had different standards for me than he did for himself and it pissed me off. I'm a grown woman, not some toddler who needs to be monitored.

One time we were running around a parking lot and Justin grabbed my shirt. I told him to hold on; I didn't want my boobs to pop out. The conversation quickly moved to how I thought women should be allowed to breastfeed in public but he didn't feel the same. He said it was inappropriate for a woman to have her boobs out, even if it was to breastfeed.

"So let me see if I understand correctly...You, a man, thinks it's not appropriate for a woman to breastfeed her child in public after a man more than likely has gotten her pregnant? After years of people over-sexualizing a woman's boobs, now it's frowned upon to use them for their actual purpose? If I ever have a kid, I'm not going to be afraid to pop my tit out and feed my child in public. And you're saying you would have a problem with that?"

"Yeah. But you could use a cover or go to the bathroom.

I don't understand why it's a big deal."

"Because you're another man trying to tell me, a woman, what I can and can't do with my body. And I'm not saying I wouldn't but I should be allowed the option. If we ever had a kid, you're saying you would think less of me for feeding your child in public?"

"I just have a lot of respect for you and want you to have that respect for yourself."

"Despite not dressing like a nun, I do respect myself, believe it or not."

"Okay. You're right, babe, you're right. Let's drop it. You're right," he said defeatedly.

The love and respect I had developed for myself felt very different from the love and respect Justin claimed he had for me. Mine was rooted in unconditional love and allowing myself to be authentic. Meanwhile, every time Justin judged me, he tried to back it up with "because I love you" or "because I respect you so much". Each time I tried to stand up for myself, the more suppressed I felt. I was expected to care more about what he thought of me rather than how I felt about myself. If someone's love requires you to hide parts of yourself, it's not love. You can't control how people see you but you can choose how you see yourself.

After the breastfeeding fight, I mentally pulled back from Justin. I was afraid of engaging with him because I didn't want either of us to spark another argument. That night he texted me: "I could really feel the love from you today." It made me happy, especially considering I had been a bit reserved. But I was glad that he was feeling more secure.

A couple hours later he texted me: "I can't sleep."

"Why not?"

"Something doesn't feel right."

"What do you mean?"

"I feel like you're holding something back. Tell me what's wrong."

"I'm confused. You just told me you were feeling the love today?"

"I lied. I wanted to see what you would say."

"I think it's childish to test your partner instead of being honest with how you're feeling."

"Oh, you think I'm childish?"

"That's not what I said. But I think testing your significant other to see if they can read your mind is childish. Also I feel I need to say this: if I have a kid, I will not be scared to breastfeed in public. If I want to wear short shorts or a revealing top, I'm allowed to do that."

"Well, I'm sorry if I don't want my girlfriend to be seen as a slut."

"And I don't like when people slut shame."

"Well if the shoe fits."

"You have a daughter. I cannot believe you're talking about women like this..."

"I just want the woman I love to be respected."

"You don't respect me unless I'm acting how you want me to act. Love is supposed to make you feel free and accepted. I feel neither and it's suffocating. You act like I am the problem. Then you expect me to be the solution to the problems you have rather than taking responsibility for how you are feeling. I think it's obvious that it's time for us to go our separate ways."

I'm like a butterfly. The more you try to pin me down, the harder I try to be free. And Justin was like a damn butterfly farmer. It had gotten unbearable with him. I felt there was no other option but to end things. The relationship was no longer good for me. After the split, I felt freer than even before we had started dating. I had gone through the lesson and was ready to fully embrace being back in a relationship with myself.

※ ·|· ※ ·|·*

My relationship with Justin definitely made me reevaluate what I need and desire in a future partner. I was hell-bent on finding someone to be with. I was more concerned with being in a relationship than I was with finding the right someone. I overlooked a lot of factors that turned out, in hindsight, to be significant to me.

The biggest thing I let slide was the vibe I had when I was around him and the energy behind how he spoke to me. He was always telling me he held me to this higher standard because he loved me and respected me "so much". His energy was almost of disapproval, like I was never going to measure up to who he wanted me to be. I think he had this precon- ceived notion of who I should be based on the type of woman he wanted to be with. I don't know if that was intentional or not but regardless of the why, I allowed myself to be placed in this suffocating box where I couldn't be my authentic self. I was dating someone who didn't respect my authentic self because *I* wasn't already respecting myself as an individual.

My habit of putting more energy into my partner than I put into my own self-growth always tried to surface while I was with Justin. Whenever I felt like I was putting more into him than myself, I would intentionally redirect some energy towards me. I was not going to let a relationship derail my journey to radical self-acceptance. I wanted to have both. But it was not working how I had hoped.

When I actively put myself first, Justin did not like that. This was a lesson I needed to learn: I was worthy of someone who loved me enough to give me the space I needed to put myself first. Being with someone who didn't respect this made me second-guess myself. Did I deserve someone who let me do things for myself? Was I worthy enough to be loved by someone who respected my desire to be a whole rather than someone's half?

I could feel myself reverting back to the girl I no longer wanted to be. I didn't want that. I had already come so far. I didn't want all the work I had done on myself to be a waste. I decided that I was going to take a year off from boys. I did not want to date. I did not want to "just talk" to some guy when there was no intention of commitment. I did not want to Netflix and chill. I did not want to have sex. I didn't even want to be approached by a guy. I was taking myself out of the game. I vowed to myself to maintain a year of celibacy.

A year with no sexy time might sound mad. Yes, it was a bit drastic, but sleeping my way through Tinder profiles was also extreme. This was my first progressive attempt at rediscovering my self-worth and loving myself unconditionally.

At the time of writing this, I've kept my promise of a year of abstinence. I feel much more empowered, loving, and happy than I ever thought I could have. A year of abstinence gave me the time and space I needed to determine what I wanted sex to mean to me. It allowed me to work through all the emotional baggage I had been carrying from my previous relationships. A year off from dating gave me the opportunity to look back on my previous relationships and revisit the lessons I learned. This past year also gave me the freedom to become the woman I've always wanted to be. Here's the Instagram post I made on my one year anniversary with myself:

> *Yesterday marked a big day for me: one year of abstinence. Last year, I went through a rough break up. After a couple weeks of reevaluating myself and what I wanted, I made a promise to myself to abstain from sex for one year. I was eager to redirect my time and energy on loving myself and evolving into the woman I was meant to become. It was easy, at first. But the more intention I put behind loving myself and growing into my highest version, the more I*

desired to quit. I realized my fear of radical self-acceptance was consistently redirecting me from the love I had within myself to a quick ego fix of sex. The closer I got to unlocking the love inside of me, my tendency was to run the other direction. Not anymore. This past year has changed me in plenty of ways but one stands out: I'm no longer afraid of my best version. I am worthy of being her. I am constantly evolving and bettering myself. I am not who I was a year ago. I am not who I was last month. I am not who I was even three hours ago. I used sex as a distraction from my self-growth but by shifting the energy I put into meaningless relationships back toward myself, I can finally say I know who I am and I LOVE HER. Self-growth and self-love are ingrained in every part of my day because I finally started putting myself first. And in that, I found my worth, my purpose, and an indescribable amount of love.

I don't know how I thought that math would work out. How could giving my body away result in gaining something, let alone my self-worth? Yes, my Fun Phase was empowering but not in a productive or inspiring way. It was my world with my rules. I had no one to answer to and no boys were toying with my heart. It was terribly gratifying. But the crash that followed was not fun.

I was projecting my lack of self-love into the world and in return, I got meaningless relationships. I was setting my bar too low. I was sacrificing things that were important for me to have in a partner because I didn't think I was worthy of finding the right man. I never felt like I deserved the man I dreamed of being with. I believed he didn't deserve me; he deserved more. I thought, *Who would want me? Some moody ex-floozy who pets every dog she sees?* But the beauty of self-love, true love, is that it is unconditional. No matter your past, self-love is always there to heal you. And you are always worthy of your own love.

Justin was a great stepping-stone for me relationship-wise. Before he and I got together, I knew I was ready for a serious relationship. I meditated and prayed on meeting someone I shared values with and could learn from and grow with. After dating him, it was the perfect chance to reevaluate what I wanted and needed in a partner. But the best part about dating Justin was he was the mirror I needed to reevaluate who I was.

Relationships are a terrific mirror, especially if they are unfulfilling. They can provide an opportunity to look within rather than outside yourself for the solution. The things I saw in Justin were traits I carried that I hadn't acknowledged and resolved within myself. For example, his lack of honest communication was highlighted because I was not always honest with myself. I didn't communicate honestly with myself about what I wanted or how I felt. And I attracted a partner who didn't do the same.

This journey of self-discovery weeded out those not meant for me. If the people around me are not supportive and excited for my growth *now*, they won't be good for me in the future. Don't keep people in your circle just because you've known them for years. Love yourself enough to create a new circle. Having a support system that believes in you will inspire you to become better.

After Justin and I broke up, I took back my freedom and started putting myself first without feeling shame. I began with journaling. It had been a long time since I had journaled. A part of me was afraid of what I was thinking, but the more I expressed myself, the more I learned about myself. I began every day with positive affirmations and every evening with a meditation. I continued unlocking the parts of my heart I had kept hidden from myself. I allowed myself to be vulnerable and embrace emotions. I wanted to heal all the parts of myself that I had been too afraid to touch. My goal was to love myself so fiercely that whoever I ended up with would know exactly how to love me through the example I was setting of loving myself.

I wanted to effortlessly express my truth, and that is this: I am worthy of everything I dream for myself.

CHAPTER SEVEN

Wisdom From The Journey

When I started college, I had no idea the path that was in store for me. Shall we do a quick recap?

My relationship with Daniel was the roughest relationship I have ever experienced. It was hard for a long time. I was convinced that perhaps we would end up together down the road. We spent two years still sleeping together, with me silently hoping to rekindle something. We never did. It took me a long time to realize I was seeing Daniel as someone I wanted to see rather than who he truly was.

He would project his internal struggles onto me, making me feel like I was the problem but also had to be the solution. And I let him because I didn't know any better. I was 19 and had a unique talent for being overly sensitive to other people's words. I didn't know my worth or how to properly love myself. I absorbed everyone's negative opinions about me and allowed them to magnify what I already disliked about myself.

So after an emotionally toxic relationship and discovering that school was no longer meant for me, I dropped out. I was a nanny over the summer, then I moved back home and got a job at a fast food place. I really wanted to perpetuate the stereotype of a college dropout. Just kidding.

I knew I was in limbo. I had dropped out of college, where opportunities magically appear for you immediately after turning your tassel. But I had no idea what my life's purpose was and I wanted to discover it before running down a path I wasn't sure was meant for me.

I was willing to change everything in order to feel at peace with myself...everything except dating that is. I was making positive changes in all areas of my life except romantic relationships. I convinced myself that this one aspect of my life would not be significant enough to hinder my growth.

Yeahhh. I was wrong.

I used romantic relationships to hide behind. They were my excuse to be lazy in my self-growth. I could throw all of my efforts into a partner when facing the unhealed parts of myself were too scary. I was more terrified of committing to *myself* than I was of committing to abusive partners, pathological liars, and guys who were less than I deserved.

After dating a string of certified dumb dumbs, I was introduced to meditation. Meditation was the key to nonjudgmentally and mindfully cultivating a loving relationship with myself. Meditation allowed me to slip into this state where I felt whole and worthy, regardless of what was going on in my life.

And the moment I felt like I had made significant progress, but still knew I had more to work through, I shifted my focus right back to dating. I entered a serious relationship with Justin, which lasted 5 months before we split up. I think part of me knew I was not ready to be in a relationship but I was a stubborn girl.

The relationship brought up a lot of conflict but it also allowed me to find immense resolution within myself. I thought a relationship would help me hide from what I didn't want to work on. Instead, my partner mirrored all the unhealed parts of myself I had been ignoring, magnifying my need to heal what I had initially tried to suppress.

This was the moment I chose to maintain a year of abstinence. I wanted to pour all of the energy and love I had into myself. I was no longer afraid of my light.

Which brings me to today, almost two years after my declaration of abstinence. I'm more in love with myself than ever.

I do want to say that no two journeys are the same. What has helped me heal and grow may not be what you need to heal and grow. I do believe that putting yourself first will have a remarkable effect on your journey. Two years later and it feels like I'm narrating someone else's story. I couldn't be more grateful for that girl promising to put me first over everything.

Along this journey I have forgiven those I didn't think I could ever forgive. I have reclaimed my health. I have healed some of the most excruciating traumas that I've carried since childhood. I have gone plant-based. I am about to become a Certified Meditation Teacher. If you had told that 19-year-old girl whose heart stopped believing in the immensity of love that she would get here, she would not have believed you. That's the power of self-love: it takes you to new heights and shows you how capable, wonderful, and worthy you are and have always been.

I want to end my story by sharing some wisdom I've

collected along the way. Now, to clarify, this is not *my* wisdom—it doesn't originate with me—but I've been fortunate enough to soak it up. Every eyebrow-raising decision I've made has had some seed of insight embedded into it. Learning to find those seeds and plant them in more fertile ground has transformed my life.

If I were to list the truths that I've uncovered on this journey, they would be:

1. Suffering does not mean something will turn out better than if it was easy.
2. Your negative thoughts (the voice of suffering) are fake news.
3. Love is the key but self-love is the master key.
4. Your intuition wants to be your friend. Cultivate that relationship.
5. How you treat yourself teaches others how to treat you.
6. Our traumas may be someone else's fault, but it is our responsibility to heal.
7. Loving yourself is not selfish. It is your birthright.
8. You are worth the effort.
9. Everyone is a mirror for everyone else. You can only see in someone what you already have within yourself. This is how we grow.
10. Everything you desire is already within yourself. No one can take it away from you; no one can cultivate for you. You are the creator of your life. This is your power.
11. Your light is instrumental to the function of this world. You are worthy of shining.

Let's look at each one of these.

Suffering does not mean something will turn out better than if it was easy.

I always thought that if a relationship wasn't difficult then it wouldn't be a great love. The more I put up with, the better I thought the relationship would turn out. But it's as Haruki Murakami said: "Pain is inevitable. Suffering is optional." I was choosing to carry around the pain, choosing to suffer, because I thought it would mature into something great. It took me a long time to realize that suffering is not constructive. It would sting at first, losing something I thought I wanted. But that pain was nothing like the agony I felt while trying to hold onto something that was not meant for me. If something is too difficult for me to hold onto, then it is not meant for me. It took me a long time to respect that realization.

If someone breaks up with you, or you break up with them, they have served their purpose in your life. That door has closed. Take time to understand the lesson and move forward. As tempting as it might be to reopen that door, silently thanking that person for lessons you learned in that relationship can save you from unnecessary drama and suffering. If there was still a lesson to be learned from that person, you would still be with them. Even then, it's not uncommon for multiple relationships to teach the same lessons. So don't justify reinvesting in a relationship claiming you want to be sure there was no lesson there or that the lesson was learned. Stay moving forward; what is truly meant for you will not pass by you, lessons included.

We are all here for different reasons and to learn different things. We all have various parts of ourselves to heal. Every person you enter into a relationship with is a catalyst for growth. From friendships, bromances, romantic relationships, familial relationships, acquaintances, strangers, everything in between...all of these people help highlight what parts of us require healing.

It all begins within us. If we forgive ourselves, we heal ourselves. When we bravely face those unhealed parts of ourselves with love and soothe our traumas, true healing begins. And when you forgive others, you still heal yourself. When you no longer feel an emotional charge towards a person or situation, then you have completely forgiven them. This is where we see the healing effects of forgiveness and lovingly letting go. This is how healing propels self-growth and self-acceptance. As we heal, we remove the layers that are no longer serving us. The more we heal, the more in tune we are with our greatest self. And our best self is the one that is healing.

What is meant for you will always bring out the good in you. If it doesn't, lovingly move on. Remove what does not inspire your evolution. Rejection, I believe, is the Universe's way of guiding you toward something or someone that *is* meant for you. This intervention is not always gentle. But it will always get its point across if you are open-minded enough to receive the guidance. The Universe is like the coach whose team you don't want to be on because they're really tough. They give you situational practice tests and push you because they see your potential. Then after you're on their team you think, *Who would I have been if I hadn't been on this team? This was meant for me!* The Universe will never steer you wrong so trust its guidance.

Your negative thoughts (the voice of suffering) are fake news.

The negative things you are currently saying to yourself sink in at a subconscious level. The more you say you have terrible hair, the more you believe it. It also works the same for positive self-talk. Your unguarded thoughts can be destructive. Very similar to toddlers, when they get sneakily quiet they're probably doing something that is not for the best. If your thoughts have been running you, they can operate silently without your consent. You might not even be aware they are being harmful. Protect yourself from your thoughts by checking in with the quality of your thoughts during the day. The next time you catch yourself saying something unkind about yourself, immediately replace it with a compliment.

It doesn't feel good to surround yourself with people who constantly put you down. Yet a majority of people practice negative self-talk in their heads all the time. Negative self-talk can be residual, stemming from being bullied or feeling unloved as a child. It could be a learned behavior from people around you who practice negative self-talk. There are a lot of places where the voice of suffering can begin. Regardless, negative self-talk and listening to this voice of suffering is self-abuse.

I'm not sure when society normalized putting yourself down but it is not healthy. There is no harm in changing your approach toward yourself. Release the need to replay negative situations over and over again. Silence the voice of suffering by replacing the negative self-talk with gentle words. When you change your thinking, you won't feel the need to recycle your experiences.

By creating a space between your thoughts and your reactions, you get a chance to evaluate your thoughts. Stop and ask yourself, "Why is this frustrating me?" Rather than looking at someone else's actions to justify our reaction, we can turn inward for the solutions. This is where you find healing and growth. You are not responsible for people's actions but you are responsible for your response to said actions. When I have come across situations that frustrate or annoy me, I have learned a lot about myself by simply asking, "Why is this situation making me feel this way?" and, "Is this how my highest and greatest self would respond to something that annoys her?" The moment you begin to notice your thoughts, you can separate yourself from them. This is you taking back your power and giving yourself the ability to deliberately change your thoughts. It just takes some effort and consistency.

Negative self-talk, or any harsh self-criticism, occurs when we are resisting change; more accurately, it occurs when we are resisting *healing* the parts of ourselves that long to be loved. Resistance is the sign that we still have healing to do. Resistance usually indicates strength but when it comes to self-healing, resistance is a virus. Resistance makes us believe that we are strong but when it comes to self-healing, it has a weakening effect. If we are against ourselves, we cannot be our solution. We must embrace the vulnerability that comes with dropping our ego, release our need to control the situation, and remain humble. Then we can bravely and effectively face the parts of ourselves that we resist healing. It is only when we acknowledge and honor the darkest parts of ourselves that we will discover our light.

This healing will cause your ego to go into panic mode. As you heal, there are going to be fewer places for the ego to surface. Squeezing the ego this hard means that the first chance it has to show up, it takes. All the places you are still healing are where the ego will pop up. I envision it like silly putty when you try to squeeze it in your hand with your fingers together, trying not to let it through. But in the words of Tag Team, *whoomp, there it is!* The ego will show up at the most inopportune times so remain aware. Your healing is the most important thing so do not let the ego take up residence in your mind and convince you otherwise.

Second-guessing yourself is the ego trying to take control so that you don't listen to your intuition. When you become aware of what still needs to be healed, you can be proactive in healing, silencing your voice of suffering, and strengthening your intuition.

You are not who others think you are. If someone tells you, "You can't do it. You won't make it. It's a pipe dream," that is a reflection of their limits, not yours. If someone tries to make you feel guilty about loving yourself, forgive them. They are simply projecting their own struggle with loving themselves. It is imperative to forgive yourself as well. You are not required to be the same person you were a year ago, a month ago, hell, even ten minutes ago. Release who you were and embrace who you are becoming: your best version. You do not have to prove your purpose or your dreams to anyone but yourself. And they are already yours, waiting for you to grab them.

Why do we feel the need to put ourselves in boxes so other people can understand us? Isn't the most important thing in life to understand yourself? I often ponder to myself, *What boxes am I putting myself in that limit me when I can be anything and everything all at once?* Self-created limitations keep us from pursuing our dreams. This idea that we have to graduate high school, graduate college, and find a job we end up hating after 20 years only to retire from said job at 65 can be a limitation. If I had known in high school I was not fat, I probably wouldn't have gained an additional 85 lbs. It was a limitation I adopted as my own even though it did not come from me. I didn't know I had the option to choose the path of healthy living because I already didn't believe I was worthy.

When you begin to meet your authentic self, you will start to recognize that many of the beliefs you once thought were organically yours, have actually originated outside of you. You might find it difficult to purge yourself of them. The beliefs that no longer resonate with you are outdated, expired, and no longer serving your highest self. By recognizing what is no longer for you, you are mindfully taking action toward ridding yourself of what has been holding you back from living your most outstanding life.

Remember back to when you were a child. Think of all the negative things other kids, friends, family members, boyfriends, girlfriends, or strangers have said to you. Maybe your parents said you weren't smart enough to get into the college you wanted, maybe your boyfriends called you a slut, kids in school called you fat or four-eyes or made fun of your acne, girlfriends disrespected you by flirting with other people... whatever it is, those comments and actions have seeped into your sweet mind even if you were not aware of them.

As children, our minds are squishy and receptive to every little thing someone says or does to us. Their words and actions are going to impact us as we get older. The intention behind how they treated you, positively or negatively, is going to pop up in adulthood, especially in relationships. There really is no such thing as a "relationship problem"; they are the mask we put on childhood traumas that have not yet been resolved and healed.

Any fears or self-consciousness that you develop as a child normally only magnifies as you get older. Personally, I wasn't taught how to work through them. As a child, I wasn't given the right tools to heal. In my case, it was because the adults in my life never learned how to do this for themselves. That's no one's fault. Every journey is going to be different. It could be years before you figure out what works for you when it comes to your own healing.

I also think our relationship problems are closely related to the connections we witnessed growing up. Maybe your parents were so in love that you knew exactly what you deserved from a partner and in a relationship. Perhaps you lived in a household where your parents did not effectively communicate, so you found it difficult to express yourself within a relationship. Maybe you grew up in a household where one of your parental figures was abusive to the other so you now attract relationships that mirror this. Perhaps you were raised in a household where one of your parents was emotionally detached, so you subconsciously search for partners who are also emotionally unavailable. The examples are endless.

The relationships I observed growing up had as deep an effect on me as the shitty things people said to me. It wasn't until I took a year off to heal that I found it wasn't just what was said to me, but what was said around me that left an impression. I was too young to grasp the adult relationship problems I witnessed. It wasn't until healing myself became a non-negotiable that I realized this had even been an obstacle.

It was like a root canal. I was confronted with the source of the majority of my suffering. The only two choices were to leave it and let it fester, or face it head on to heal the pain. The ache was so great that I had to be proactive in curing it. I did a meet and greet with all my old narratives and my suffering. It was painful. I had to honor what I had been through, and what I had attached myself to, in order to grow from here. I had to actively pass out forgiveness to those, who in my mind, were in the wrong. And I had to forgive myself.

Holding onto a grudge takes more effort than forgiveness. Forgiveness may not feel good but a moment of giving yourself peace is infinitely healthier than sipping the poison of a grudge for years. It's like carrying around a hundred pound backpack you personally picked out. I was too stubborn to drop mine when it was no longer serving me. Grudges against your old self can show up as rereading your old narratives. Your old narratives are like the 1st edition of a textbook. But your self-growth, self-love, and self-acceptance produce the 11th edition of said textbook. The old one is no longer of use to you. You have already gotten what you needed from it so lovingly put it away.

It took months to work through my deep-rooted suffering. I mastered a forgiveness exercise that has become invaluable to my healing. I normally do this while meditating, but you could do it anytime. I close my eyes and picture in front of me whoever I need to forgive. And depending on how upset I am with the person or situation, I say, "I forgive you," and shut an imaginary door behind me. More often than not, this exercise starts with me yelling at whomever is in my mind's eye and then slamming the imaginary door as hard as I can. I continue to do this exercise over and over until I am able to genuinely say, "I forgive you," and I gently and lovingly shut the door behind me. When there was no emotional charge connected to a memory or person, that's when I found I had completely forgiven them. This forgiveness exercise gave me my power back. All I needed to do was let go of my self-created attachment to the other person or belief. And I was free.

Love is the key but self-love is the master key.

Old Me thought romantic relationships and sex were the only keys to cure any pain. I took it upon myself to try and heal the people I dated, especially when they had no interest in improving themselves. And I used relationships and sex as routes to circumvent my own healing, thinking I would make my way to myself eventually.

Love between human beings, especially when it's healthy, is beautiful. But self-love is where all of that beauty truly originates.

Humans are fluid and constantly evolving. Loving yourself unreservedly is where the magic of radical self-acceptance and the superpower of self-love flourish. And when you love all of you, even your shadow side, you have the power to love others with that same ferocity. By loving someone unconditionally, you are giving them the space and freedom to be who they need to be in any given moment. Loving without expectations will support others in becoming their best self on their own terms. It is our right and responsibility to do what will make this world a better place.

It is important to remember not to force this healing on someone who is not ready for it. We must respect each person's journey because none will be identical to ours. This work toward radical self-acceptance and restoration will only begin within you. The focus must remain on you. Your light will inspire others to look within themselves and rediscover their own radiance. This healing work you are doing for yourself *is* the catalyst for change. By fiercely loving yourself, that fire will encourage others to do the same. Everyone is a lighthouse; we just have to remember to turn on our light for others.

You cannot be committed to your suffering and to your healing. We begin to heal ourselves by forgiving those who let their suffering manifest into ours. A great visualization I use for letting go of what no longer serves me is letting go of a balloon. In the balloon, I envision muck, bitterness, pain, and anything else that I need to release. Oftentimes there is a person in there as well. I visualize all of the negative energy flowing down my arm, out of my hand, up the balloon string, and settling into the balloon. Once it's all outside of me and in the balloon, I let it go. The balloon drifts off and I'm free of the weight I had placed in it. But forgiveness is not always a one-and-done. Anytime the pain comes back up, it's time to practice forgiveness again. Until the memory comes up without attachment or aversion, there is still healing to be done.

An important step toward radical self-love is to stop being your own enemy. There's an African proverb that says, "When there is no enemy within, the enemies outside cannot hurt you." When we love ourselves unconditionally, no outside opinion will have a hold over us. When you abandon yourself, you open the door to self-abuse. This self-abuse distorts your mind into thinking the only validation available to you is external.

I was on a desperate search for someone to love me because I was afraid to love myself. I dated person after person, maintaining relationship after relationship, one-night-stand after one-night-stand, trying to fill this void that *I* created. I cultivated this feeling of lack within myself yet I was looking for someone else to fix it. I bullied myself into believing that I was not worthy of what I dreamed for. I was over-thinking and overanalyzing. All this did was make me unhappy. This over-thinking and overcompensating in relationships came from a fear of being alone.

Just for the sake of saying so, you *can* heal while in a relationship. The right partner will give you the space you need to heal. They will not cause you anxiety but give you a peaceful and safe place to be yourself. I know plenty of people who have started relationships, aware of their own shit, and were able to cultivate loving and healthy connections. On the other hand, I know a lot of folks who prefer to do their healing work before finding a partner. Neither is better than the other. Doing what is best for you now is what will be best for you in the long run. Whether you are in a relationship or not, remain self-aware and practice honest, intentional communication. Nothing changes the fact that you are, and have always been, capable and worthy of healing.

**Your intuition wants to be your friend.
Cultivate that relationship.**

Intuition, beyond being a gift we are all born with, is something we must cultivate. It is unable to grow if we leave it untended. Our intuition holds all of the answers we will ever need. If we ignore our intuition, constantly following others' words of advice, our own inner voice gets more and more quiet. But your intuition wants a deep relationship with you.

Oftentimes we are so in our heads, trying to reason things out in our minds, that we may forget to listen to our gut/heart space. The issue we face when we do start listening is that intuition and fear are both gut feelings. How do we know if the voice we hear is our intuition or if it's fear?

Intuition propels you forward from your heart space. Your soul already knows where it's going even if you struggle with trusting its directions. But fear keeps you in place; fear loves the familiar. Fear might even move you farther from where your soul yearns to be.

Fear can be useful; for instance, say you're face to face with a grizzly bear while camping or someone has just broken into your home. Or perhaps you experience fear the day before you start a new job. The fear that comes from our natural fight-or-flight response has a purpose. It wants to keep us safe. But when it comes to our dreams and desires, fear is really good at masking itself as intuition.

Intuition is gentle, neutral, and does not rush you to make a decision. Intuition has an unnaturally calm tone, given that it is guiding you toward the frightening unknown. But your intuition always knows what is best for you, even if you can't see it with your own two eyes. Fear, on the other hand, is emotionally intense, and generally steers you towards the dead end of "and then I'm going to be poor and starve to death", or whatever else represents your worst-case scenario. Fear might convince you that not making a move is better than trying. Fear likes stagnation. Fear is like the backseat driver who claims they aren't a control-freak but the second you get on the road they can't stop worrying and suggest going back home.

Your intuition and fear are two different voices no matter how similar they may sometimes sound. And if you have trouble differentiating between the two, that is your signal to strengthen the relationship you have with your intuition. Confusion is an adverse reaction to being out of alignment with your intuition and your highest self. If you are confused, that is an indication you are entertaining fear and not your intuition. Another sign that you are operating from a place of fear is failing to grow spiritually. If you feel dormant concerning your personal growth, chances are you are in a fear cycle.

Remember that intuition has no emotional charge; it simply guides you to what is best for you, regardless of your perception of how things should play out. The more you tune in to both your fear and intuition, the more clearly you'll be able to tell them apart.

Your intuition wants to be your closest friend. It never leaves you no matter how much you might ignore it. It wants what is best for you even if you doubt its suggestions. The more I leaned into my gut feelings, the easier it was to see the contrast between how my fear and intuition communicate with me. As I actively listened to my fear and my intuition separately, I found it easier to tell them apart whenever a gut feeling did pop up.

Are any of you familiar with the Yanni vs Laurel debate? It's this audio illusion sound clip. When you play it, you either hear *Yanni* or *Laurel*. Well, people lost it. People couldn't understand how their friends couldn't hear what they heard. Some people, myself included, heard one and then the more they listened to the clip they would hear the other. Eventually linguists and audiologists spoke up about how the sound waves you create when you talk can make you predisposed to what you hear. They also said if you are surrounded by people who speak with a higher frequency (higher pitched voices) as opposed to a lower frequency (lower pitched voices), then your ears are inclined to hear either the higher-pitched *Yanni* sound, and vice versa. I'm usually surrounded by women, so it made complete sense why I heard *Yanni*. My ears are used to hearing those tones so they naturally gravitated toward listening to them.

It works the same way with your intuition and your fear. They both have different frequencies. If you have been listening to one over the other, it is normal to gravitate toward listening to the first one you recognize. It is possible to have listened to fear for so long that when it speaks up, the tone is so familiar you feel comforted by it. And the same goes for your intuition. The more vulnerable you are willing to be with *both* your fear and intuition, the less effort you will need in recognizing them.

You fear requires compassion; it is just trying to keep you safe, even if that means keeping you in a box that is no longer serving you. When you become aware of all your fears, you will know immediately if it is your fear popping in for a chat or if it is your intuition giving you guidance.

Your intuition is one of your greatest superpowers. Intuition is the internal compass we all have. All it does is point the way. It doesn't berate you if you go the wrong direction. No matter how lost or off course you've gone, the needle gently shows you which way to go. No lecture. No questions as to why you didn't listen. It has no physical evidence that everything *is always* working out for your greatest good. And although you don't know where exactly it's pointing or what you'll encounter along the way, you know you can trust its directions. In that moment of divine surrender and trust you are allowing the magic of life to embrace you.

How you treat yourself teaches others how to treat you.

The universal golden rule seems to be: "Treat others the way you want to be treated." We're taught the phrase as kids and grow up with it as an internal compass. But I'd like to shift our perspective on this sentiment.

There is a beautiful symmetry when you invert this statement. Treat *yourself* the way you want others to treat you. It's easy to fixate on how others treat us but I want to take a step back and look at how we are treating ourselves.

Only when you treat yourself with unconditional love, respect, and compassion, can you truly embody those qualities for others. It is impossible to speak unkindly to yourself and then turn around and genuinely speak kindly to, and about, others. It is unreasonable to be dishonest with yourself and expect others to trust you. It is hypocritical to hold others to a higher standard than you hold yourself.

You are allowed to speak kindly to yourself. You are allowed to get a pedicure. You are allowed to be proud of yourself. You are allowed to wink at yourself as you pass by that store front window. You are allowed to love yourself! Self-care is not vain or selfish. When you put yourself first, you are better able to serve others as your best self. What we are not already doing for or giving to ourselves, we cannot require someone else to do or give. And your approach toward others is a direct reflection of how you are currently treating yourself. It all begins with you being self-aware of your tendencies. You are the starting point and also the end game.

There are going to be people who treat you like shit for no apparent reason. These people are running on autopilot. They have treated themselves the same way for years and years so it comes naturally to them to be hateful, judgmental, and abrasive. When you come across these people, please show them compassion. Oftentimes people who are rude to themselves externalize that hostility to magnify and justify what they are already feeling. They are looking for people outside of them to verify their emotions. Imagine how miserable those people must be, walking around with so little love for themselves that they act out to make other people validate their perception. May we meet these people with the love and compassion they are starving themselves of.

We are the light-workers. It is time to illuminate those who have forsaken their own light.

Let's look back at the trust example. If we aren't honoring our intuition but we expect others to trust our intuition and advice, there is a disparity between who we are and who we would like to be. It is not fair to, consciously or subconsciously, pressure others to act toward us in a different way than we act toward ourselves. We cannot look outside of ourselves to heal. If we treat ourselves as victims, as people who are unable to grow and heal, the world will see the same. And that is so far from the truth.

You are a walking miracle. You are already whole. You are already worthy of healing and releasing what no longer serves you. You are already worthy of respect. You are already deserving of love, peace, joy, and abundance. These are your birthrights. Take responsibility for how you behave toward yourself. Recognize all that greatness within yourself first. If you don't already acknowledge it, you are giving away the superpower that is radical self-acceptance. You are providing people with blindfolds so they are unable to see how great you are.

I've been there. I was the girl who would dim my light the moment any positive attention was on me. My voice of suffering was a raging bitch at that time. I wouldn't allow others to see me as better than I saw myself. I would choose partners who maintained my self-constructed box to keep me from growing, healing, and loving myself. I abandoned myself. I treated myself like shit. I was so unhappy and felt unworthy of self-love. I am the personal architect of my life and I was creating a personal dystopia in which I was unfixable and unlovable. How I felt about myself was the only lens I could see through. When I stopped acknowledging my light, it made it easier for the world around me to do the same. I hid my magic from myself and ended up hiding it from the world as well.

Years later I have found the relationship that matters most (aside from the relationship with Universe/Source/God/the Divine) is the relationship you have with yourself. We all have a light within us and as we love ourselves unconditionally, we won't be seeking someone else to keep us illuminated. I know from experience it seems easier to search for that external validation, that external love, thinking that it will solve all your self-love issues, but it won't. Because no matter how long and hard you search outside of yourself for it, no amount of outside love can replace the magic that comes from loving yourself. External love will never be enough; but *you* are enough. It all begins within. You are one in a damn billion, baby. It's time to treat yourself like the walking wonder you are.

Our traumas may be someone else's fault, but it is our responsibility to heal.

It is a great self-teaching tool to hold yourself accountable for any parts of yourself that still need to be healed. Your divine purpose is hidden in the unhealed parts of yourself. It is scary to have to face the deepest parts of yourself. But healing those neglected elements is how the most impressive growth will occur.

A lot of people don't want to self-heal because they enjoy having someone else to blame for their problems. Yes, many of our traumas can be traced back to a person or a situation but it is not their responsibility to heal you. If you are aware enough to acknowledge the parts of yourself that need healing, then you are the only one with the power to facilitate that healing.

You have to be willing to look objectively at yourself, without judgment, to see the parts of you that need to heal. This takes an incredible amount of courage and vulnerability.

I've noticed that a lot of people tend to hold onto their childhood traumas because it gives them someone to blame. I was one of those people at the beginning of my journey. It was easy to blame my parents, family, kids at school, ex-boyfriends, even strangers for how I felt. It was years before I realized if I have the capability to figure out how my childhood traumas are manifesting in my present, then I must take responsibility for healing them.

People can only give what they have been given or what they have cultivated themselves. If your parents were never taught how to love themselves, and they never found the tools to love themselves, you can't hold that against them. If someone has ever purposefully made fun of you or made you doubt your worth, I urge you to recognize they are projecting their insecurities onto you. It is not personal. Negativity clings to negativity. People will try to put you down for a multitude of reasons. And if we compare our journey to another's, we are creating our own setbacks. This is why self-love is so fundamental and important.

Comparison is what kills your dreams. You think you aren't good enough? Compared to whom? You could get a handwritten letter from God saying, "You're on the right path! Keep going!" and one trivial person could make you doubt it. I would attach my self-worth onto things that went wrong but never things that went right. Limiting beliefs rely on you to compare yourself to others to feed their false agenda.

Remember that your limiting beliefs are fake news. You are allowed to achieve everything you desire for yourself with ease. Trust that what is meant for you will not pass by you.

When people around you are out of alignment with their highest self, they will try to bring you out of alignment with them, intentionally or not. They may make you distrust what you're doing. They may make you doubt your journey to healing, self-acceptance, and self-love. Take back the power you're giving others to make you second-guess your greatness. The net is always there, ready for you to jump. And the beauty is that the Universe will never take the net away. But why worry about the net when you have wings? You have always been destined to soar.

Loving yourself is not selfish. It is your birthright.

I want you to think of three things you love the most in the world. I'll wait.

Many of you are thinking: friends, family, significant

other, my dog/cat/bird, the internet, oxygen, water, mac and cheese (vegan of course), my phone, music, meditation, coffee, my car, my computer. This list could go on. You've got three things in your mind that you love so much you could not possibly live without them. Be honest: how many of you put yourself on that list?

It's overly common to put oneself last because we *choose* to put other things in front of us. It's no wonder why one of the most common fears someone has is the fear of being alone. We don't know how to be alone. We don't know how, or are afraid to, put ourselves first. We love our family, friends, pets, food, electronics...And yet when we list things we love, we tend to leave ourselves off the list. Let's stop this trend right now. You are worthy of your own effort and love.

I have always battled between giving and preserving my energy. It took me years to understand not everyone is deserving of my time and energy. No one was entitled to either. If it is coming from a loving place, it's okay to be protective of your energy. This is how we create healthy boundaries. You are allowed to have boundaries; they are signs of self-respect and self-love.

We are all banks of energy. You may find yourself loaning out energy and never having it returned. This was my experience. I gave and gave and gave, rarely ever receiving anything in return. Through this constant giving, I lost myself. I lost my will. I lost my self-respect. I diminished my self-love. I was constantly looking for the return from those I had given to, unaware of the eternal spark of love inside me. I've been on this journey for years. The turning point only occurred within the last year and a half. That was when I started looking within for answers rather than outside myself. I was finally letting myself access the everlasting glow of love that replenishes without question or judgment.

Over this last year and a half, I have overcome a lot of mental limitations I had put on myself. I've worked through the voice of suffering, which is arguably so common that people might not realize it's something they *can* surrender. I've done a lot of work on myself and yet there's one thing that always catches me: giving without expectations. There are plenty of times I can give free from attachment. And then there are some instances where I give, and suddenly crave thanks or acknowledgment. I was conditioned from a young age to desire recognition. When I don't receive the praise I expected, I immediately feel the need to withdraw back into myself. The moments where I feel this hunger to be seen, heard, and appreciated is my sign that I still have healing to do. I need to be pouring more love into myself.

One can't pour from an empty cup. It is okay to put yourself first. There is nothing wrong with healing and self-care. I had quieted my inner child who told me giving free of expectation brought joy. Rather, I began listening to the adults who made it seem like joy could only be achieved through receiving. Joy is not sustainable through external validation. Joy must first be discovered from within. Inside is where we find fulfillment, satisfaction, and replenishment.

My self-sacrificing only highlighted that I didn't know how to properly love myself. I was aware of this. And yet I continued to put other people in front of me. I thought that by loving someone else wholeheartedly, it would mirror back and I would learn to love myself with the same, satisfying love. But I discovered, rather slowly, that I could not fully love another person before completely loving myself. I could only give what I was already giving myself. And because I didn't fully love myself, there was no way someone else would be able to love me the way I desired.

You are your greatest obstacle but you are also your greatest solution. You can be your greatest fan and still be your greatest enemy. When you don't care about yourself, you suffer. When you care too much about how others perceive you, you suffer. When you ignore your needs and desires, you start to believe that you aren't worthy of those things. We all deserve to treat ourselves better.

You are not worth what you think you are. You are worth so much more! When you reclaim your worth and recognize your greatness, you will easily and naturally raise your standards. Don't be worried about how this internal shift will affect those around you. Raising your standards will only scare away who and what was not meant for you in the first place.

Contrary to popular belief, it is not a requirement of your existence to struggle with loving yourself. You were not created to overcome some great self-esteem issue. You were made whole, exactly as you are. Somewhere along the way, society has pressured everyone to have some kind of internal challenge that they feel the need to overcome in life before they can be happy. But life isn't meant to be a struggle.

I dislike the idea that we are born having to climb up this giant ladder as we age to reach some artificial precipice that has been forced on us. It is your divine right to love yourself; the struggle was never meant to be a part of this. You are not obligated to dislike yourself. You do not have to feel guilty for already loving yourself. You were created for this purpose. All the love you've ever needed is already inside you. Outsiders will try to convince you this journey should be based on a need for admiration, recognition, or external validation. But loving yourself is the real prize and we are all worthy of this.

You are worth the effort.

Change is uncomfortable. But from my experience, not loving and trusting myself was even more uncomfortable. The turning question for me was would I rather be vulnerable in learning to love myself or maintain the trauma of not fully loving myself? Through this vulnerability, I gained empowerment and a level of self-respect I didn't know was available to me. Knowing my worth is not a negative thing. In fact it is one of the most loving things I could do for myself. Everyone deserves to know how worthy they are of happiness, peace, and love.

Attachment and love are not synonymous. We need to move away from this idea that having a partner is the priority. *You* are the priority. Your worth is not dependent on whether or not you have a partner. Your purpose cannot be defined by what other people say or think about you. You are the only person who can define your purpose. By trusting yourself and your journey, you are harnessing your power.

This empowerment will show our purpose: to heal ourselves completely. When we heal, we gain radical self-acceptance and master unconditional self-love. When we heal ourselves, we are becoming one with our greatest selves.

This healing work is not as glamorous as people might believe it to be. It's not all love and light and euphoria. Healing can feel heavy, unpleasant, and awkward. Healing is being willing to open up your emotional bruises, immerse yourself in the vulnerability, and free yourself of the suffering you've carried. Allow yourself to fully feel and do not be ashamed of it. One of the greatest services you can give this world is being honest and transparent in all aspects of your journey. This includes the unfortunate parts. Now is the time to trust yourself. Trust the timing. Embrace the uncertainty and the fear. Enjoy the beauty of healing and becoming because anything is always possible. You are worth the effort. You are worthy of it all.

**Everyone is a mirror for everyone else.
You can only see in someone what you already have
within yourself. This is how we grow.**

Doesn't it seem like there are some people who just enjoy being miserable? They are so intimate with unhappiness that they will never be content with anything else.

These people may project what they are feeling as being your fault. In reality they are being faced with a part of them that hasn't been healed. You are their mirror. In you, they see what secrets reside in their souls.

We say we want to change but when faced with the opportunity, so many of us slow down, scared. Don't be afraid to free yourself from the pain you've carried for so long. When it comes to suffering, everyone has a choice. One can play the victim, content to blame their own suffering on someone else. Or they can be brave in releasing the pain that is no longer serving them without blaming anyone. Sure, it would be easier to avoid this work but I don't believe that will help heal this world.

I have found when I am living fully in my truth, the most healing occurs. When I am connected to my highest self and dousing myself with love, I feel restored. Instead of ignoring the collective suffering going on in the world around us, maybe we should start facing it head on. We are all responsible for healing ourselves. If we do this, if we begin within, others' healing is inevitable.

I always have the power to wish others peace, happiness, and a life without suffering. Everyone is carrying some weight. If we purposefully withhold love with the guise of teaching someone a lesson, we've just handed them more weight. It did not inspire them to release what they are struggling with. Giving pain will not heal yours. Now is the time to drop all the expectations we have for others and simply love them for who they are in any given moment. When we can silence our ego and lead with our soul, love comes out. It becomes easier to wish others well rather than push our expectations onto them. Love inspires people to be better.

Judgment, on the other hand, is not inspiring. We project

what we don't want to feel onto other people. And when we judge others, we are often also judging ourselves. Judgment of the self is us abandoning our best self. Judgment does not inspire change. Judgment is not encouraging. It is constricting. I created further mental separation by putting people in boxes. This did not promote healing in my life. And it sure as hell did not stimulate healing in those around me. When I stopped putting myself in a box, I found it was natural to not put others in a box. It was instinctive to allow people the space to grow.

I learned to hold space for everyone around me to be exactly who they need to be in any given moment. This is an intentional practice that I still work on. I'm not perfect but I do try to purposefully approach everyone the same way, accepting them as they are.

One day a friend said to me, "That's what I love about you. You accept me and love me for exactly who I am!" I was flattered but all I could think was, *Duh, because you're radiant and honest and real.* I replayed this moment in my head, wondering if other people felt I loved them for exactly who they are. And I realized this was not always the case.

Sometimes our egos cloud our minds. They might convince us someone isn't authentic or kind, simply because we are comparing them to ourselves. I always expected a lot from people because I expected a lot from myself.

I have to give everyone the same amount of space to be whoever they need to be. I have to give people the same space to be pleasant or angry or rude or excited. The beauty of healing is that it is not our job to decide who mends, when, and how. All we are called to do is hold space and remain supportive.

It is a superpower to allow others to be, without judgment or attachment. All journeys are different. We must respect the path that others choose to be on, even if we wouldn't have chosen it for them. The best gift we can give others is to hold a space for them to be whoever they need to be. Whoever they are in any given moment is who they need to be in order to become their best self. By meeting people where they are, we bridge the self-created gap of separation. You didn't create their life's blueprints. You are not responsible for another person's journey. You are only responsible for your own journey and that is what will inspire.

And while we hold space for others, your highest self is holding space for you. I always compare it to a friend saving my seat in the theater. She knows I'll show up, regardless of how many previews I miss or how late into the movie I arrive. She saved my seat because she knew I would make it. This happens over and over, film after film, lesson after lesson. Some days, I'll only miss one preview. Some days, I arrive early enough to grab some popcorn. Other days, I make it at the end credits. But my highest self never judges me on when I arrive because at least I am arriving. She only ever congratulates me because I always choose to show up for myself.

This is how I gauge how in alignment I am with my highest self. Sometimes we show up at the same time and there are times where I'm so late I miss the movie entirely. But my highest self is always there, patiently waiting for me.

I still experience these lags between my soon-to-be old self and the woman I am meant to become. The more I align with my greatest self, the less distance I feel between the two. This whole process taught me to be gentle with other people just as my highest self is gentle and patient with me.

Everyone acts differently so we can all be catalysts for each other; catalysts for change, healing, and growth. We need to allow others to spark our self-awareness. We need to be willing to look at ourselves and our actions from a 30,000 foot perspective. This broad view allows us to see what we might normally ignore if we only choose to heal one part of ourselves rather than our whole selves. Keep yourself in check so that your only option is self-reflection, growth, and self-acceptance. The only competition you should be in is with the old you.

**Everything you desire is already within yourself.
No one can take it away from you; no one can cultivate for you. You are the creator of your life. This is your power.**

How do I cultivate the greatest amount of joy? When I enter situations sans expectations or attachments to the outcomes, my ability to experience joy multiplies. I'm not saying this is easy. This is a practice that I have to actively work on and sometimes still forget. When I was young, I never went outside to play with the expectation to find fun. I simply went outside to play and the fun was inevitable.

As I got older, my expectations expanded. I cared more about others' reactions to me rather than how I felt about myself. I was attached to the idea that external validation would tell me whether things were going well or not. This influenced me to only give when I knew it would be well-received. This contributed me to giving less. I became easily hooked by my emotions when what I expected of others didn't align with how they reacted. I started disconnecting from the Universe, thinking that I wasn't doing anything right. This led to closing off my heart. And down the rabbit hole I went.

A large component of my struggle with self-love stems from my expectations not being fulfilled. I assumed that everyone had the same thought processes as I did. I expected everyone to respond to me in the ways that I would have responded to them. I would get emotionally invested in their responses, which often led to more disappointment and self-doubt. If I made dinner for my partner, I would get upset if they didn't say thank you. I was giving strictly with the intention of receiving something in return. I was conditioned to perform based on expectations. And I only had high expectations of other people because I had high expectations of myself. This was the projection.

The reason people feel so easily drained is because they expect others to validate them rather than fulfilling themselves from within. When you expect something from someone else, you are giving them power. But everything you are searching for is already within you. You are the creator and curator of your life. Everything you cultivate within yourself will manifest in your external world. Believe you are worthy of receiving all the good and you will. Remember the most important step: begin within.

Your light is instrumental to the function of this world. You are worthy of shining.

I envision this infinite flame of self-love within every person on this planet. There's this eternal flame within us we get to tote around for life. I believe the goal is for everyone to help illuminate this world in love. I'm sure we can all agree the easiest way to do this would be to tend and grow our own fire. Yet not everyone is aware of the infinite light inside of them. Regardless of whether or not they are aware, it is always there. And it will never abandon them.

For those who have discovered their flame, it's easier to keep it lit. These people look to themselves for fulfillment rather than outside of themselves. If their flame dwindles, they are self-aware enough to light it up again from within. Then there are those who are aware of their infinite fire but not utilizing it. And there are those who are completely unfamiliar with their flame. These people are only looking externally for someone or something to ignite them.

I fell in the middle category. I walked around, semi-aware of the light inside me, but chose to look for someone else to fulfill me. I was waiting for the people around me to help nourish and sustain my flame of self-love. And if it went out, which was often, I felt lost and hopeless. I was afraid of healing myself and being self-sufficient. This immense love inside of me was uncharted territory. I was more comfortable allowing myself to dim rather than access and cultivate my own spark.

I wanted to be a lighthouse for people to see how self-love could illuminate their souls. But my actions were not aligning with who I wanted to become. It took a lot of dedication to learn how to rekindle my own fire. I had to catch myself when the habit of searching externally would pop up. Now, I'm best friends with my flame. I know exactly how to relight my candle from my eternal embers of self-love. There's no turnaround. If I get dumped or feel the need for some self-care, those needs are immediately satisfied. When you are both the giver and the receiver of your own love, it's a magic that you will never stray from.

It's a common misconception to think that by putting yourself first you are putting everyone else last. That is not true at all. When you put yourself first, you are becoming your best version. That is how you are better able to serve and love this world. When you love all parts of yourself, it becomes effortless to love the world around you. When you heal yourself, that healing is reflected out into the world. You can't heal a broken leg without ultimately healing your body as a whole at the same time. Self-love is the catalyst not only for healing ourselves but for healing this world. Each time someone heals a past trauma, a light is flicked on. And you can see that light in the people around you. This encourages more and more people to begin their self-healing journey. By authentically and courageously being gentle with the parts of ourselves that we have been at war with, we are illuminating this world, flame by flame.

Afterword

This is the end of *this* story. But of course, it's not the end of *my* story. My days of self-destruction have shifted into a time of self-discovering divinity. And that time of discovery will never end.

For the longest time I was terrified of healing my heart. I didn't believe I was worthy. My voice of suffering was on repeat in my head and I allowed it to control my life. I hid from my best self behind relationships. I figured if I was able to cultivate a romantic relationship then I would be able to, indirectly, heal myself. That was my coping mechanism to get out of the hard work it would take to heal. I was putting off the inevitable because it provided me with immediate and tangible results; results that never lasted and never satisfied the ache I felt from my lack of self-acceptance and self-love.

If anyone had told that girl back in 2011 the beautiful adventure that was in store for her she would not have believed them. She was a girl who was hooked on narratives that no longer served her and dismissed her intuition. A girl who rejected her magic and dimmed her light. A girl who forgot to believe in the infinity of her own love. And I can't thank that girl enough for being brave in getting me here. I have so much gratitude for her and abundant appreciation for everything she has gone through.

The moment I stopped searching outside of myself for the answers, I found everything I was looking for and more. I discovered myself and the woman I was always destined to be.

This journey has been like climbing a mountain. Looking ahead at the daunting task of learning to love and accept myself unconditionally was intimidating. And I knew two things: 1) this was going to be the hardest thing I had ever done and 2) it was going to be the most rewarding expedition I would ever embark on.

I had to learn to trust my gut. I tripped often, gaining scars and wisdom along the way. I encountered unexpected turns, pop quizzes, fear, stalls, and uncertainty. But every time I worked through a lesson or released an old narrative, I felt like I leveled up, gaining new perspective not only on what I had overcome but what I was headed toward. I discovered my life purpose. I mastered forgiveness. I gained radical self-acceptance and unconditional self-love.

Now I am manifesting the life I have always dreamed of. And none of this means my journey is over. I'm not perfect. I still slip and struggle. I still have so much I can learn. All that matters is I keep my promise to continue progressing in all areas of my life. I am committed to loving myself, my healing, and my vision of a renewed world.

Honor the space your highest self is holding for you by stepping into it. Step into your power. Own your light. Your spark is an essential component to the restoration of yourself and this world. We already contain the magic we wish to see. This is your sign to begin within. You are the wonder this world has been waiting for.

Acknowledgments

I hold an infinite amount of gratitude for every person who helped this book come to life. From the characters in my story to the divinely curated team behind this project, I am so thankful for you all.

Thank you to my family for supporting me and for being the best first audience a girl could ask for.

Thank you to my dear friends who have accepted and loved me even when I struggled to do so for myself. You are all beyond wonderful and I'm so grateful for you. To my two best girlfriends, Amber and Emily: there are not enough words in the world to describe the adoration I have for both of you. You have been there for me from the beginning and I am so damn lucky to have you as my best friends.

Immense gratitude to my editor, Kristin van Vloten, for inviting me to lean into vulnerability while writing. Thank you for encouraging me to trust my voice and my story. I am so fortunate to have had you as my editor. You are this book's fairy godmother.

A huge thank you to The Self Publishing Agency for their guidance and generosity while writing this book. And a special thank you to Megan Watt for taking on a first-time writer. I guarantee this book would still be on my Google Drive without you.

Thank you to Mia Ohki for the breathtaking cover and illustration. I am so honored that you designed my cover. Your work will forever have me in awe.

Thank you to Laura Wrubleski for being pure magic and creating the most stunning book interior I could ever imagine. You are a true gem.

And finally, eternal gratitude to Sah D'Simone. Thank you for guiding me through the most transformational time in my life. You were the lighthouse I needed to find my way back to my best self. Thank you for shining your light; it inspired me to rediscover my own.

14339166R00090

Made in the USA
Lexington, KY
06 November 2018